HECKINGTON
A
JOURNEY THROUGH TIME

By
Heckington Village Trust

Printed by
Albert Gait Ltd.
Victoria Street,
Grimsby.
DN31 1PY

Production management by Langhan Print Associates,
Milton House, Willingham Road, Knaith Park, Gainsborough, Lincolnshire, DN21 5ET

All rights reserved. Reproduction by any means including photocopying, or storage in any retrieval system whether mechanical, electric, electronic, or by photoelectric or by other means without prior written permission of the copyright holder's assigns or successors in title is strictly forbidden except for the purpose of comment or review.

Copyright © 2001
Heckington Village Trust

ISBN 0-9541065-0-4

PUBLISHED
BY
HECKINGTON VILLAGE TRUST
HECKINGTON, LINCOLNSHIRE, ENGLAND

HECKINGTON: A JOURNEY THROUGH TIME

Chapter 1.　　Early Heckington: The Land and the Sea..7

Chapter 2.　　Medieval Heckington: A Place with an Identity...............................16

Chapter 3.　　Tudors and Stuarts: Wealth and Poverty Side by Side......................27

Chapter 4.　　1700-1850: From a Watery World to a Modern World....................39

Chapter 5.　　1850 onwards: Victorian Heckington..56

Chapter 6.　　The Second World War..90

Chapter 7.　　A Walk Round the Village...102

ACKNOWLEDGEMENTS

Producing a book of this nature cannot be achieved without the help and co-operation of a large number of people. Therefore we will attempt below to acknowledge those who contributed to its publication.

Our thanks to the Local Heritage Initiative comprising the Heritage Lottery Fund, Nationwide and The Countryside Agency who awarded the generous grant that enabled us to finance the printing.

I suppose the ones who have put the most actual manual labour into the research are the members of the fieldwalking group past and present, who over the last thirty years or so have tramped up and down the land around the village looking for the evidence of the past. Then, when the weather was unfit standing up to their elbows in icy water washing and identifying the finds many of which have proved to be important in piecing together the early history of the village. Of course none of this would have been possible if it hadn't been for the goodwill and cooperation of the local farmers and landowners to whom we are extremely grateful.

There are many residents of the village past and present who, over the years have given freely of their knowledge and experience. Harold Cook and Miss P.Lowth being two who in the past were great contributors. We are grateful also to Richard Mowberry for his exquisite sketches and Charles Mowberry for his information. Also Rosie Teasdale for her internet historical research.

Many members of the Village Trust have worked particularly hard over the years, none more so than the late Irene Zealand whose first hand local knowledge and photographic collection were invaluable.

Thanks also to Robin Bush, Sid Money and Eileen Robson who, together with many others have donated photographs and information over the years. This brings us to Mr Michael Cole Sumners who probably took the first photographs of Heckington back in the early eighteen sixties, but for him and others like him such as Benny Smith our heritage would be a lot less comprehensive.

Mr and Mrs Michael Brown have given valuable assistance by allowing access to the archives of the Sleaford Gazette, also David Start and the staff of Heritage Lincolnshire and the National Monuments Records Department. Information and help from Hilary Healey and together with Brian Simmons permission to use drawings and photographs from their publications.

Sleaford Library and in particular Julia Dabbs gave a tremendous amount of help and encouragement. Lincolnshire Libraries, the Lincolnshire Archives, The Usher Gallery Lincoln and Cecil Higgins Art Gallery Bedford, England also supplied valuable help and information. Thanks also to the Reverend David Boutle, to Doctor Michael Elliot and The Wyberton book publication group. Also the computer expertise of Charles Raphael of ACS Sleaford.

INTRODUCTION

Ever since the 1970s and the publication of the book "Heckington in the 1870s" by the Village Trust there has been an underlying thought that one day the Heritage group would produce an overall history of the village. A great deal of information gathered at that time was put to one side for future use and over the years more and more research has been done. Contributions have come from many sources and from many local people. A great many hours have been spent by members of the group specialising in different timeframes and trawling through the dusty records of various archives. However a place such as Heckington has so much history that there comes a time when a decision has to be made about publication or the research would go on indefinitely with no end result. Thus, about two years ago the group decided that it was time to work towards the production of a history of Heckington from the earliest times.

With so many *village history books* now available why write another one? Partly pride, because we want our village to be represented. Partly because Heckington has a long and interesting history, a story that is worth telling. Mainly because Heckington has seen tremendous changes through more than five thousand years of history, but has always provided a home for its inhabitants.

If you climb the Church Tower in Heckington and look out across the surrounding countryside, almost everything you will see is either directly man-made or the incidental result of centuries of human activity. This is true not only of the buildings within the village itself, but also the hedges, the field boundaries, the roads, the dykes and drains, the trees and crops, and the whole pattern of the landscape. So the early history of the village is about how this tale of transformation began. It is about the first people to settle down in the place we now call *"Heckington"*. It is about how those people began to make a living from the land and from the sea that swept in much closer to the village than now; and it is about the way their activities set in motion a chain of events which has created the environment we live in today. We hope this book will lead to a greater understanding of the ever changing nature of village life and a deeper appreciation of the value of the community. It is as much a handbook for the future as a record of the past.

Heckington Village Trust
Heritage Group.

This book has been researched, written, designed and compiled by the Heckington Village Trust Heritage Group which is comprised of:

In alphabetical order

Pat Banister

George Keeping

Charles Pinchbeck

Lesley Pinchbeck

Sandra Sardeson

Kevin Teasdale

It has been a team effort with each member contributing his or her skills to the building up of the finished product.

The photographs have been taken by conventional film cameras as well as digital camera and scanned in or downloaded to Adobe Photoshop 5.5 where they were processed and sized for importation into the Adobe Pagemaker 6.5 publishing program. The text has been typed and processed in Microsoft Word by each contributor, committed to disk, edited and transferred to a central computer for compilation, to present to the printers ready for the press.

We have done our utmost to ensure that all the facts presented in this book are correct according to our sources. However mistakes can be made and it is for this reason that a further reading section is provided at the end of the book. We have also taken great care to try and spell names correctly and apologise to anyone whose name is incorrect.

CHAPTER ONE

EARLY HECKINGTON
THE LAND AND THE SEA

Looking out over the rolling flat lands of the fens from the tower of Saint Andrew's Church, Heckington, it is not difficult to imagine how it would have looked over four thousand years ago.
Photograph taken by Kevin Teasdale.

It will probably come as a surprise to many current inhabitants of the village to learn that in Roman times salt-water creeks came in from the Wash as far as Heckington. Two thousand years ago the land between Heckington and Boston was marsh interspersed with islands of higher ground and a constantly changing pattern of salt water flooding in from the North Sea. A major local industry was salt making! As you travel on the current A17 towards Boston, in a field on the left just beyond the Garwick café, keen eyes can still see traces of reddish debris. On closer examination these turn out to be fragments of the clay vessels that were used in Roman times and earlier to evaporate the water from the creek, leaving behind the valuable salt

The dark patches left by the debris from the salterns can be clearly seen.
Photograph by George Keeping.

Heckington is one of a line of fen-edge villages stretching down to Bourne, all lying on a ridge of high ground beyond which the land falls away to the east. This may be hard to believe if you always use a car to drive into Heckington, but any cyclist will soon tell you that you have to pedal uphill to get into the village from the main road. Indeed if you go down the Howell Road and then turn left towards Ewerby and Asgarby you will clearly see the land dipping into a valley before rising up as you reach Heckington with the spire of the church dominating the landscape. In these days of worries about global warming and flooding we may have good cause to be thankful to the Bronze Age, Iron Age and Roman settlers, who were equally troubled by the thought of rising water and so chose their place to live with great care.

The valley and the bypass run beyond the hedge in the distance, with the land then rising up to the village. The wooded slope to the east (left) can be seen clearly with the Church dominating the horizon. Photograph, P.Banister.

Not only did Heckington stand on rising ground but it also offered fresh water, both from the Wash Dyke, known to most villagers nowadays as The Beck, together with a sufficiently high water table to make it relatively easy to put down wells in the main village for drinking water. The very name of nearby Howell means 'Holy Well' and shows how important water sources were in earlier times. As well as water there was good arable land nearby for growing crops and safe pasture for cattle and sheep on the edge of the fen. The fen itself would have been quite different from now, perhaps with a series of creeks running out to the Wash and a marshland environment that created a haven for fish and wild fowl, both of which would have been important extra sources of food. We know that over the last few thousand years the climate and the coastline in eastern England have changed radically. In Bronze Age and Roman times the weather seems to have been mild and wet and the sea would regularly break in from the Wash, before the colder climate of medieval times and the drainage operations of later centuries led to the recession of the sea and drying out of the fenland as we know it today.

The Wash Dyke as it is today snaking off towards the east. Probably not in quite the same position as in earlier times. It may have been moved a little further north.
Photographed by Kevin Teasdale.

FIELD WALKING

The reason we know about salt making in Heckington is because of a survey of the fields conducted by field walkers that started in the 1970s and is still continuing today. Many people think that the only way you can find evidence of the past in the fields is to dig or use a metal detector. Not true! If you are interested in the history of the village, as opposed to hoping to find an unlikely treasure trove, you need look no further than the surface. The majority of the surrounding fields still contain a scatter of typically grey pottery fragments brought to the surface by the ploughing each year. These date from Roman times and are nearly two thousand years old. The bad news is that a cracked fragment of a Roman cooking pot is not worth any money, since it really is not all that unusual. What it tells us is that this part of Lincolnshire was heavily settled in Roman times by people who lived in well-made houses and who farmed the surrounding land just as we do now. Any pots broken as a result of everyday use were thrown away into the crew yard with the manure from the animals. This was later deposited onto the fields to improve the soil for crop growing and to make life more interesting for modern field walkers on a cold winter's day.

THE EARLIEST SETTLERS

Hunters and their families will have gone up and down the hill that Heckington now stands upon for as long as human beings have colonised this part of Europe. These people left no written records behind them, nor did they build lasting houses that left identifiable debris in the ground today. But they did leave behind some of their tools and these still tell the tale of their presence.

These tools were little pieces of flint with sharp edges that were used as knife blades for cutting and piercing. The land around Heckington is naturally rich in sharp black flint, as digging in any local garden will soon reveal. The fieldwalking group have found pre-historic flints which have been shaped into arrowheads, scraping tools and knives. Some of the pieces of flint are even cracked and crinkled as if they had been subject to extremes of temperature. In fact early hunters may well have placed these pieces on their fires and then thrown them into their pots in order to heat up the water for cooking.

A very fine flint blade found by the fieldwalkers and photographed by George Keeping.

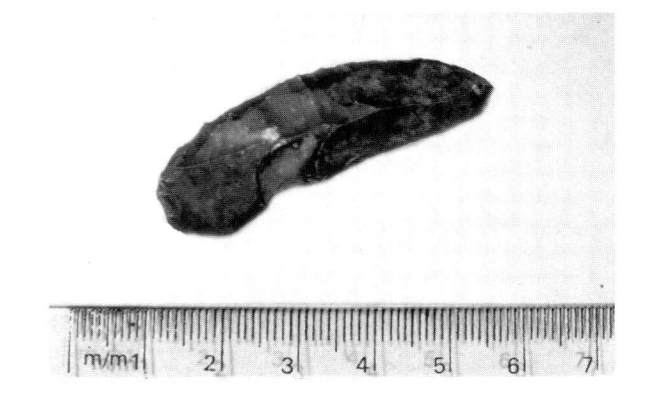

Although we know from flint and pottery that people were making use of the local resources for their tool making, the first settlers in our area were not cut off from the rest of the country. In a field near Side Bar Lane off the A17 one of the field-walking group found a stone axe-head brought to the surface by recent ploughing. Experts at Nottingham University have conclusively identified this axe-head as coming from Langdale in Cumbria and dating from perhaps 2000 BC. Langdale in the Lake District has a seam of fine-grained, grey-green volcanic stone that was extremely hard and could be worked into a very sharp edge. Good implements like this were very valuable to the first settlers for clearing woodland, so a primitive 'factory' was established at Langdale which traded its wares far and wide. It was one of the products of this ancient factory that was found at Side Bar Lane.

A view of Langdale in the Lake District. The ancient axe factory was high up on the escarpment marked by the white downward streak on the left of the rock face. Photographed by George Keeping.

Alongside stone tools, the first metal tools began to be used during the years between 2600 and 700 BC, which are known as the Bronze Age. Bronze is a mixture of one-part tin to eight-parts copper and could be cast into sharp and hardwearing tools or hunting weapons. Bronze age finds from the fields around Heckington and adjacent parishes have included flat metal axes, socketed axes and a distinctive spearhead. It is not hard to imagine the spear being used to catch fish or birds in the marshy fenland and perhaps finally lost over the side of a boat by a careless fisherman. The field walkers have also found a scatter of Bronze Age pottery, which is typically dark on one side, sandy yellow on the other, and very well fired. Most of this pottery has appeared in fields in Heckington Fen, particularly in an area close to Sandy Lees Lane. Salt making is also likely to have made Heckington a place of settlement in the Bronze Age and subsequently in the Iron Age, which is usually taken as the period from 700BC to the Roman invasion in 43AD. The demand for salt may have arisen from a fashionable taste for salty food, but more probably related to increasing livestock farming and a growing need to preserve, store and trade meat.

The magnificent bronze spearhead found by Mark Sardeson near the Wash Dyke and photographed by George Keeping.

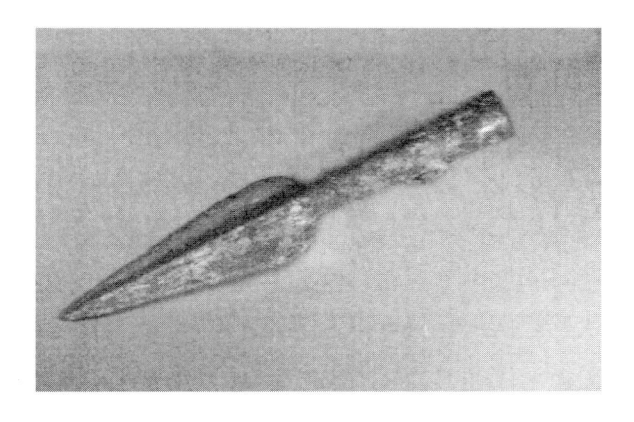

Left; the stone axehead manufactured at Langdale in Cumbria. Found in a field down Side Bar Lane and photographed by George Keeping.

So the history of settlement in the area around our present village goes back long before the Romans. We have evidence from finding tools and pottery that surprisingly sophisticated people were living, farming, pursuing industry and trading here. It was probably the existence of dry land on a hill close to salt marshes that first led people to make their mark on the landscape. That mark is still visible in aerial photographs of a site in Heckington Fen which has a distinctive boundary and is a scheduled ancient monument that has yet to be excavated. It may represent the earliest farm in the village and may even date from 1500 BC, which is about the time of the siege of Troy.

FLINT-WORKING

Quite a lot is known about how flints were worked. The usual technique is known to archaeologists as hard-hammer percussion, which simply means hitting one rock with another. One larger piece of flint was the core and another smaller piece was the hammer. The object was to use the hammer to knock razor-sharp flakes of flint off the core, which could then be used on their own or mounted on wooden implements as knife blades. The edges of the core would be left with a characteristic pattern where the flakes have been chipped off and could also be used as a scraping implement itself. The cores and flakes found on the fields around the village are quite distinctive and could not be made by anything other than human hands. In the Italian Alps the preserved body of an Ice Age Man was recently found, with roughly worked flints still in his pockets. So we must suppose that our ancestors would carry a supply of flints with them and then improve on them during the long, dark winter evenings.

ROMAN HECKINGTON

Although Julius Caesar landed twice in Britain in the years 55 and 54 BC, the real Roman occupation of Britain was the result of an invasion in 43 AD when the Roman general Aulus Plautius headed a force of about 40,000 men. The Roman military machine was so successful that the Emperor Claudius himself came to Britain and personally led the army into Colchester to accept the surrender of eleven British kings. From there, the legions quickly overran the land up to and beyond the Wash. Lincoln was soon established as the most important Roman settlement in our area, with a road system that brought Roman influence directly into our parish.

A Roman soldier kitted out for travel with about three days rations in his backpack. His uniform consisted of his helmet (Cassis), shoulder and breast armour made of metal strips (Iorica Segmentata), woollen tunic (Cingulum), javelin (Pilum), short sword (Gladius) [hence Gladiator], curved shield (Scutum) and his leather sandals (Caliga). However we suspect that heavy cloaks may have been worn at times in the British climate.

Heckington seems to have been a busy and wealthy place in Roman times. A major civil engineering project took place nearby, with the construction of the Car Dyke, which ran all along the Fen Edge. It still exists to this day. It plays its part in land drainage, running as a dyke from Sandy Lees Lane down to the A17, crossing the main road and disappearing along the line of the modern single-track road into Great Hale Fen. The purpose of the Car Dyke has been much debated. The current view is that it was primarily a drainage channel to catch water running off the higher ground and lead it out into the main creeks in the fenland. It therefore served to dry the land close to the high ground and make it more suitable for arable crops or permanent pasture. However, the Romans were resourceful people and the Car Dyke was probably also used for local transport of heavy goods that would have been hard to move by land.

Although some parts of the Car Dyke are silted up and almost filled in many stretches are still doing the job it was originally built for as photographed here down Heckington fen by G.Keeping.

The evidence from the fields shows how trade expanded under the Romans to provide materials for an increasingly sophisticated society. Finds in the parish have included not only mortar pots made in the Nene valley near Peterborough but also fine red Samian pottery imported from the continent. There may have been several villas for the wealthier inhabitants of Roman Heckington. Certainly one stood in the field beyond the modern railway line at the end of Banks Lane. It was roofed with heavy red clay tiles like the ones made in the Roman kiln at the Car Dyke and supported on what must have been a really solid framework of roof timbers. This suggests that areas of the country were still heavily wooded in Roman times. On the field where the villa once stood, field walkers have also found *'hypocaust'* tiles. These were used as a central heating system. Some of them formed columns beneath the floors of the villa to allow the under floor heating to circulate. Others were hollow box tiles that carried the hot air up inside the walls of the house. Life in Roman Heckington must have been quite comfortable if you could afford a slave to keep the fire well-stoked. In addition there is a scatter across the villa site of Roman pottery and tile fragments, which have been cut down into small cubes. These are known as 'tesserae' and will have been used to make mosaic floors for the most important rooms in the villa.

Other evidence of Roman lifestyle includes many fragments of cooking pots made from typically Roman grey-coloured pottery and deposits of oyster shells. Oysters were a favourite Roman delicacy and again suggest that the sea came in closer to the village than nowadays.

A general view of the excavated tile kilns near the Car Dyke. It is of brick construction and it is assumed that the sides would be arched to form the capping. Its overall internal dimensions are twelve feet four inches (3.76 metres) by two feet five inches (0.74 metres).
Photograph taken from Roman tile kilns at Heckington by permission of B.B.Simmons.

Field Walking Techniques
The survey is carried out by field walkers, small groups of disreputable-looking individuals to be seen tramping across muddy fields on Sunday mornings in the middle of winter, their heads cast down as they search for tiny pieces of pottery, tile or flint on the surface of the ploughed land. The technique is a little more sophisticated than this suggests, involving gaining permission from the owners to walk the land, dividing the fields into 10 metre strips and walking in a straight line to sample what can be seen on the surface. The finds are then taken back to the walkers' houses to be washed and dried. On days when it is too wet or too cold to go out they meet and examine their finds, dating and marking them, while entering the hard-won results on a computer for future generations to study.

Everyone knows that the Romans loved building roads and it is possible that we have one of our own in Heckington, running out into the fen, to the south of Littleworth Drove. There is evidence from aerial photographs that there were Roman farmsteads out on the very edge of today's fen with a wide scatter of small bits of grey pottery across the fields. We certainly should not assume that the village we know today has always been the most important settlement in the area. For example, large amounts of Roman pottery have been found close to the Garwick café on the A17 heading towards East Heckington. The name *'Garwick'* was certainly used for this area in medieval times and the site is just a little higher than the surrounding farmland.

In Roman times it may have been an island of permanent dry land beyond the Car Dyke and within the salty marshes of the fens. The importance of salt in flavouring food and preserving meat has already been mentioned. If you look carefully at some of the clay fragments of salt-making troughs found just beyond Garwick, you can still see Roman fingerprints visible on them! They form a striking reminder that real people lived here two thousand years ago, in a place where we race by in our cars and where they once pursued an industry on the bank of a salt-water creek.

Left; fieldwalkers with heads down and eyes glued to the ground looking back into history. Photograph by G.Keeping.

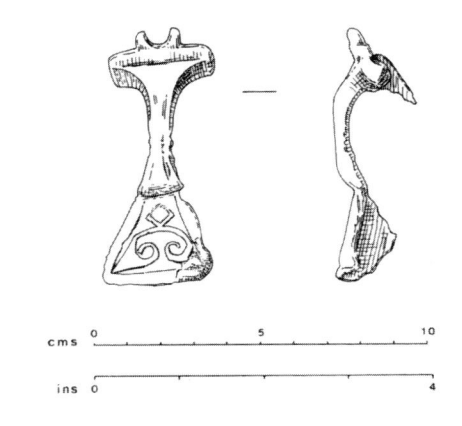

Above; a brooch. One of a collection of illustrations of finds in the vicinity of the tile kilns. Drawn by Hilary Healey for Roman tile kilns at Heckington, Lincs.

The five different types of Roman tiles represented on the tile kiln site near the Car Dyke.
Photograph taken from Roman tile kilns at Heckington Lincs by permission of B.B.Simmons.

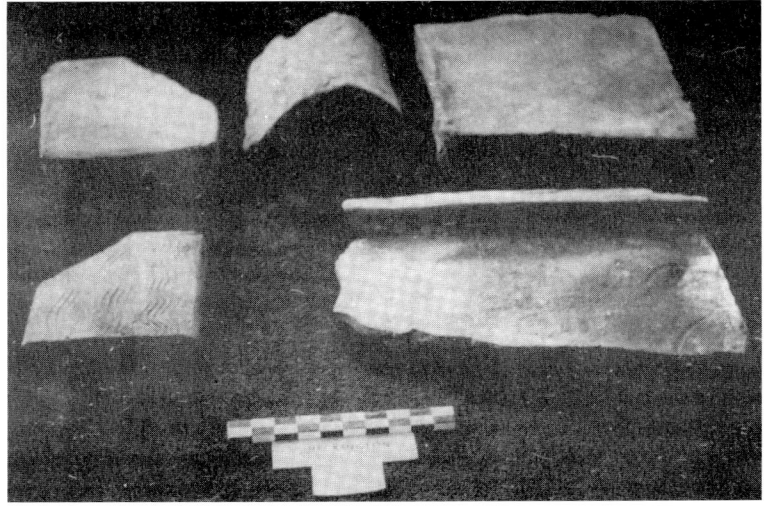

CHAPTER TWO

MEDIEVAL HECKINGTON: A PLACE WITH AN IDENTITY

The settlements in Roman time were spread across a wide area of the parish, with homesteads close to farmland rather than necessarily concentrated in the present day village centre. So although the Romans made their mark on the landscape with roads and drainage schemes, the identity of Heckington as we know it was not really established until Anglo-Saxon and medieval times.

The Anglo-Saxon period from about AD 400 to the Norman Conquest in 1066 was a formative time for Heckington. The Saxons are known as village settlers and it is quite likely that the main village site we have today is essentially their creation. We cannot be sure of this because modern householders are surprisingly reluctant to allow archaeologists to dig up the centre of the village to find the evidence! However we know that around nearby Butts Hill beside Station Road there were Saxon burials and Saxon pottery has been found at Garwick in reasonable quantities. Early Saxon pottery is dark grey, hand-made and contains small pieces of quartz, mica and other minerals which sparkle distinctively when held up to the light. Compared with the Roman pottery found in the same fields it appears crude and less well made. It is perhaps a reminder that we cannot take it for granted that civilisation always advances from age to age.

Looking to the west across Butts Hill from Station Road before the Miller's Way housing development. Photographed in 1998 by Pat Banister.

However, we do at least owe the name of our village to the Saxon and probably also to the Viking invaders who began to land in the north east of England in increasing numbers over eleven hundred years ago. The village is recorded in the Domesday Book of 1086 as both *'Echintune'* and *'Hechintone.'* The more familiar *'Heckyngton'* first appears on a document in 1115. These variations in the early spellings may not be significant but they do give an idea of the pronunciation.

THE NAME OF HECKINGTON

In the past people have speculated that the name may derive from a plantation of *'ash'* trees, still one of the most common tree in our hedgerows. Modern scholarly opinion, however, is that the name means *'Heca's village.'* The word *'ton'* is Anglo-Saxon for a homestead, whereas *'Heca'* is almost certainly a Danish personal name. So there may have been an early Saxon settlement on our site, which was later taken over by Danish settlers. Written records confirm that in 877 a division of the invading Viking army partitioned the ancient Saxon kingdom of Mercia and made settlements in the area known as the Kingdom of the Five Boroughs, namely Derby, Leicester, Nottingham, Stamford and Lincoln. So it is possible that this was the time when the village gained its current name. As well as veterans from the Viking army, there must been immigrant farmers from Denmark because of the remarkable number of Danish words still recognisable in local place and field names, including *'beck'* - meaning a stream, *'garth'* - an enclosure, *'holme'* - high ground in a marsh, and *'ing'* - a meadow or pasture.

THE DOMESDAY BOOK

The Domesday survey of 1086 provides clear evidence that the land was divided between existing Saxon farmers and the Norman incomers. The Bishop of Lincoln held some land in the parish, as did a Norman named Wido de Creon. The lord of the manor was Gilbert de Gant, who came over with William the Conqueror and was actually related to the king by marriage. Gilbert and his family were technically tenants-in-chief of the manor rather than owners, as the Norman kings claimed ownership of all the land for themselves. Domesday tells us that the Normans did not completely supplant the existing local families since Saxons named Colsein, Tarchil and Algon are all recorded as important landholders in the local area.

An impression of what Heckington could have looked like at the time. Viewed from the south and looking over what would become Cobham Hall, up the hill towards the Church of the time.

The fields are farmed in strips and the houses of the serfs and villeins are built near the land they work.

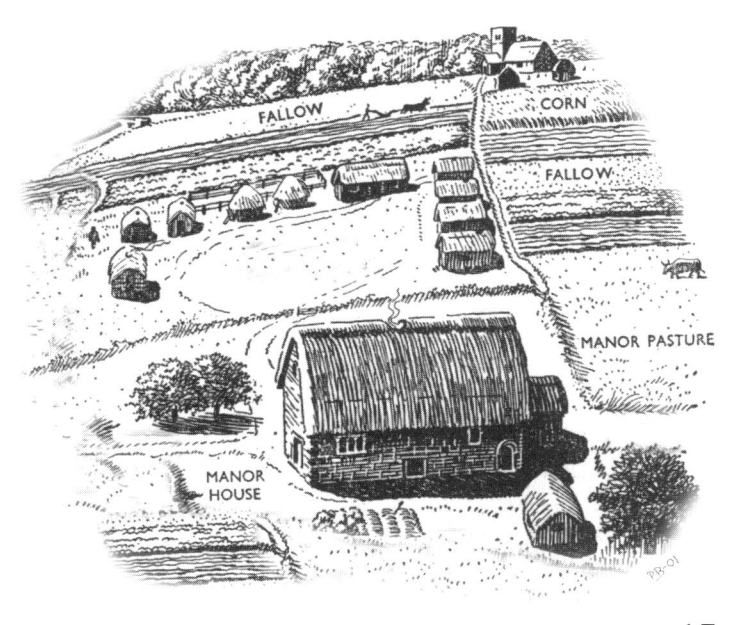

THE FARMING WAY OF LIFE

By 1066 the settlements were probably established where they are now, with the pattern based on the village of Heckington with outlying large houses at Garwick and Winkhill. There is a good scatter of medieval pottery across all the fields probably introduced by manuring, indicating large scale livestock holding. However the greatest evidence about the farming way of life in the medieval village is rapidly disappearing from our sight.

If you go down Cameron Street, crossing the road with care at the Old School, and continue along the second half of Cameron street to stand on the stile, a quick look at the grass field facing you will reveal a surface that rises and falls in an even pattern. The dips or *'furrows'* are the remains of ancient medieval strip farming, which will have formed the pattern of all the arable fields around the village. Almost everyone in the village at one time will have used some of these strips for growing crops for their own use and to sell at local markets, with the ridges between the furrows acting as markers to stop strip holders arguing over the boundary between their plots. The furrows will have gradually grown deeper and the ridges higher as a result of years of ploughing by teams of oxen. Farming must have been a more sociable occupation in those days, with people constantly crossing the fields to move from one strip to another, offering plenty of opportunities to stop for a chat.

Go over the stile at the eastern end of Cameron Street and walk down the public footpath. The evidence of the ridge and furrow ploughing is plain to see. Tom is standing in the sunken roadway to give a sense of scale. The undulations can be seen along the hedge bottom.
Photograph by P.Banister.

Records from the Village Trust field survey in the 1970s show far more remains of ridge and furrow than can be seen in the ploughed fields of the new millennium. Modern tractors are more efficient than teams of oxen and wheat or oil seed rape are easier to crop if the fields are level. So ridge and furrow persists only on fields that are more or less permanently down to pasture. Even so, medieval ideas can still influence modern thinking. The division of the modern allotments on Boston Road is clearly based on the idea of a medieval strip, although the tenants make do with wooden posts to indicate their boundaries and disputes are mostly confined to arguments over the depredations of stinging bees and man-eating dogs.

The allotments on Boston Road, showing the width of the plots similar to medieval strip farming in the open fields.
Photograph by Kevin Teasdale

THE FEUDAL SYSTEM

In the middle ages, the tenants-in-chief will have held large numbers of strips scattered across the village fields. They will have rented out some of their strips to freemen in the village in return for cash payments or payments in kind. But the poorer people in the community were known as 'serfs' or 'villeins.' The lord of the manor and other large landholders allowed the serfs to hold some strips in return for services. In the main this meant that serfs had to labour on the lord's fields for certain days a week. In this way the lord of the manor had his fields ploughed, sown and cropped without needing to pay wages, but could sell the resulting produce to get money and grow richer. After the Black Death came to England in 1348 and the infection wiped out up to a third of the population, the feudal system began to break down. There was a shortage of serfs to farm the fields and the ones who remained began to use their bargaining power to receive payment for their work. So the economic laws of supply and demand seem to have operated then in much the same way as now.

AN AGE OF FAITH

The Anglo-Saxons were Christians, and the Viking settlers soon converted, so there will have been places of worship in the village long before the Norman invasion. However the first date for a building we can be sure about is 1086 when a church and priest are recorded in Heckington. There is a tradition that this early Saxon church was replaced by one in the Norman style in 1101-4 at a cost of £433. This church was in turn replaced by our own much more magnificent building in the years between 1300 and about 1333. This church, now called St Andrew's, was described in Victorian guidebooks as the *'Queen of the Fens'* and is one of the finest medieval churches in the country. So how has it come about that such a remarkable building was erected in this particular village?

The answer includes a royal visit to the village and the hatching of a murder plot to seize control of the government of the country. The detail was unearthed through the patient researches of Charles Kightly and the story begins on 10th April 1309 with the death in Heckington of Lady Lora de Gant. Lady Lora and her late husband Sir Gilbert held the lordship of the manor, having been in the family since 1086. Their marriage was childless, so with Lady Lora's death the lordship and all their Heckington lands passed to the King of England. In 1309 that king was Edward II, a man with a reputation as a weak and spendthrift monarch whose defeat at Bannockburn lost any last vestiges of English control over Scotland. Like all politicians, Edward used patronage to try to reward those who were loyal to him and among the most loyal of his friends was Lord Henry de Beaumont. Lord Henry was second cousin to the king and had grown up with him. In October 1309 Edward therefore rewarded Henry with the Heckington estates of the de Gants, making Henry the new lord of the manor and putting in place the first piece in our jigsaw.

By coincidence, the patronage of the church of Heckington fell into the hands of the king at the same time as the de Gant lands. In the early fourteenth century the abbey of Bardney, near Lincoln, had the right to appoint vicars in Heckington. However, in 1309 the rector of Heckington died at a time when the abbey of Bardney was without an abbot and so could not make an appointment. It will come as no surprise to find that this meant that control of the church once again fell to the king, who quickly appointed a priest from his own court named Richard de Potesgrave.

The tomb of Richard de Potesgrave in Heckington Church showing the damage later inflicted during the troubled times of the Civil War. Photographed in 1999 by P.Banister.

Richard de Potesgrave probably came from the village of Potsgrove near Leighton Buzzard and we know his parents' names were John and Juliana, because he later funded a chantry chapel in Heckington to pray for their souls. He is described in documents as the king's *'chaplain.'*

Although this will have involved some religious duties in the royal chapel, it also meant writing the king's letters and being what we would nowadays call a career civil servant. In medieval times, the clergy were the experts in reading, writing and mathematics and as such were recruited by the government to run their administration. They were ideal officers of the government, since they could be rewarded out of the revenues of the church, without obliging the king to dip into his own pockets. Moreover, since as priests they were not allowed to marry, these medieval civil servants could not legitimately build up dynasties of their own nor hand down their offices to their children.

We can only imagine how the medieval inhabitants of Heckington must have reacted to the arrival of not just one, but two wealthy new residents who were personal friends of the king himself. Did they mutter darkly about incomers from the south with no understanding of Lincolnshire ways? Or did they boast at Sleaford market of how they enjoyed catching up on court gossip when they went to call on their new neighbours?

Beaumont and Potesgrave did not spend all their time in the village. Beaumont acquired lands in Folkingham where he built himself a castle, although Heckington seems to have been the administrative centre of his estates. Potesgrave was with the king in 1321 at the siege of Leeds Castle in Kent when Edward II overthrew his enemies and executed thirteen of the castle defenders on the spot. Potesgrave must have played his part in the conflict, since he was promptly rewarded with keepership of some of the lands confiscated from the rebels. Nevertheless, Heckington still retained its attractions for him and it is recorded that about this time he acquired a house and garden adjacent to the rectory in preparation for his eventual retirement.

Potesgrave's interest in Heckington did not stop there however. A new village church was already beginning to take shape. The architectural evidence shows that it was built in two phases. The early part was the nave, or main body of the church, and the north crossing that projects out into the churchyard facing Cameron Street. These were probably built in the ten years leading up to 1309 and were partly funded by Lady Lora de Gant. However, it is the second phase of the building, which created the magnificent church we admire today. The building plan for the tower, the south crossing that faces St Andrew's Street and the chancel probably commenced in 1315. Heckington's two royal courtiers, Henry Beaumont and Richard de Potesgrave, funded this second phase.

Heckington church is unusual in that it was built over a relatively short period of time and architecturally represents the high point of the Decorated style with magnificent flowing tracery in the main windows, particularly the east window of the chancel. This is enhanced by the sumptuous chancel fittings: the Easter Sepulchre, which held a crucifix and host that were watched over from Good Friday to their unveiling on Easter Sunday; the sedilia where the priest, deacon and sub-deacon would sit during some parts of the High Mass; the double piscina where they would wash their hands and the sacred vessels; and the founder's tomb, where Richard de Potesgrave now lies at rest. The quality of the work on these fittings is extraordinary and could only have been afforded by wealthy and well-connected men such as Beaumont and Potesgrave.

The magnificent Easter Sepulchre reckoned to be one of the finest in the country. It is made of different stone from the rest of the Church and it is generally agreed that it was manufactured somewhere else and transported and erected here in sections. A plaster cast was made of it and displayed at the Great Exhibition in Crystal Palace in 1851.
It depicts the Risen Christ, the women at the Tomb and the Angels.
Information taken from "The Parish Church of Saint Andrew, Heckington" by Reverend D.C.Speedy.
Photo P.Banister 1999.

A ROYAL VISIT

Edward II, patron of the two courtiers, had his reign cut short by a successful rebellion led by his wife, Isabella, and her lover, Roger Mortimer. Edward was imprisoned and almost certainly murdered in 1327. Beaumont declared his opposition to Isabella and Mortimer and fled for his life into exile in France. Potesgrave was called upon to do one last service for his old master, organising Edward's funeral and burial in Gloucester Cathedral. The official story was that Edward had died of natural causes and his young son was crowned as Edward III, while the real power in the land resided with Isabella and Mortimer. Richard de Potesgrave decided to retire from this turbulent court and came back to Heckington to supervise the final phase of the building of the church. He must surely have thought his part in national politics was at an end.

Then one summer three years later, the villagers must have been surprised to hear a fanfare and see a party of richly dressed lords and ladies coming up the hill to Heckington. How much more extraordinary to see the royal standard flying at the head of the column and in the centre of the throng a fit young man of eighteen with a military bearing. This was Edward III king of England and for three days from August 19th to August 21st 1330 he held court in Heckington.

The villagers were told that he had come to visit their magnificent new church and doubtless they were not surprised that this remarkable building should be worthy of the attention of a king. Richard de Potesgrave would have officiated at High Mass and surely must have put his house and belongings at the disposal of the king during his stay. But three days was a long time, even for a visit to a church like ours, and we can only wonder whether rumours of a different motive for the king's stay in Heckington emerged at the time.

Edward III (1312-1377) one of England's medieval warrior kings and father to the Black Prince. The photograph, courtesy of the National Gallery, is of the gilt-bronze effigy in Westminster Abbey. It shows Edward as an old man, long after his visit to Heckington.

Edward III and Potesgrave must have talked about the life and death of Edward's father. Significantly, Potesgrave would have seen the body of the dead king when he went to arrange the funeral and would also have talked to people who had been close-by when he died. Edward III must have suspected that his mother and her lover had murdered his father. Did he come to Potesgrave for confirmation of his worst fears, under cover of a visit to a fine new church? We cannot know what was said, but Edward's subsequent actions suggest he found an answer to his question. Only two months after his visit to Heckington, on the night of 19th October 1330, the young king entered Nottingham Castle with an armed guard and arrested Isabella and Mortimer. Isabella was packed off into retirement, while Mortimer was promptly dispatched to the scaffold. Soon afterwards Beaumont returned from exile and Potesgrave had his royal grants renewed, presumably for services rendered. The church was completed in fine style and Richard de Potesgrave lived on in the village until his remarkable life came to a close in 1349 at the great age, for those times, of about seventy-five years. He is remembered now for his tomb in the chancel that he had built and in Potesgrave Way, one of the newer streets in a village still dominated by his own great church.

This is a view of the east window that would be difficult to take now due to the growth of the trees. The photograph was taken just after the restoration of the roof in 1867 by Michael Cole Sumners.

A LOCAL TAX SCAM

What we know about medieval Heckington is very patchy and there is much more to be discovered by anyone with the time and ability to cope with medieval Latin records. But for now, there is one more story concerning the village from published sources that is worth reconstructing. It starts with a four-line court record published by the Lincoln Record Society:

"Roger de Wollesthorp, Henry de Tideswell and Thomas de Strouston and Robert de Assheburne, their deputies, on 12th September 1337 extorted four stones three and a half pounds of wool in excess of the accepted weight from the vill of Heckington".

To make sense of this short record we need to take stock of what was happening on the national scene at the time. Richard de Potesgrave was still alive in 1337 and Edward III had become a war hero. The king had already led an English army to the continent and started creating a European Union of his own by conquering large parts of France and modern Belgium. However, wars were very expensive and Edward had to persuade Parliament to vote him a wool tax to pay for them. This tax allowed him to requisition a specified number of sacks of wool from villages in the main wool producing counties, which he could then re-sell to raise cash for the war effort. Lincolnshire was one of the most important wool producing counties in England and so the King appointed wool collectors to go to each village and weigh out a proportion of their wool to be taken away as payment of the tax.

Sheep shearing in medieval times. Wool was one of the most important sources of wealth in eastern England in the middle ages, with flocks of sheep far outnumbering the human population.

The job of wool collector must have been as unpopular in the fourteenth century as that of income tax inspector is nowadays. However, the wool collecting job did have its compensations. As well as being paid for touring the country and weighing out the wool, the Lincolnshire wool collectors seem to have hit on a way of making a little extra on the side by fiddling the weights they used on their scales. This meant that they took more wool than they should from the villagers and re-sold the extra for their own personal profit, rather than the king's.

On occasion they supplemented this even more by extorting extra money from the poor villagers to get them off their backs. What is more, four of the wool collectors seem to have run this racket in every village they came to, not only Heckington but Great Hale and Little Hale, Burton Pedwardine, Ewerby, Asgarby, Quarrington, Sleaford, South Kyme and Helpringham - and all on the same day! They were at least hard working men. But what they did not count on was the fact that on market days people from the different villages came together and compared notes about what they had been up to. Soon the whole county was in uproar at the depredations of the wool collectors so that Edward was forced to cut short his military campaign on the continent and come back to England. He set up a special inquest with trusted judges to take statements from all the villages and then take action against the crooked tax collectors.

Lawyers discussing a case in a medieval court, from the Piccolomini Library in Siena.

In the end, the law seems to have caught up with most of them. Wollesthorp, Tideswell and Strouston pleaded guilty in 1341, asking for a catalogue of similar offences to be taken into consideration. They were imprisoned in Lincoln and obliged to pay a hefty fine to secure their release. Robert de Assheburne never turned up at the hearing. He was declared an outlaw and sadly we hear no more about him. Still it seems that even in medieval times the rule of law worked in our part of the county, even if justice was no quicker then than in modern times.

The pattern of medieval strip farming is still clearly visible in this fine example from an aerial photograph.

CHAPTER THREE

TUDORS AND STUARTS: WEALTH AND POVERTY SIDE BY SIDE

It has been said of Lincolnshire in Tudor and Stuart times that no county had worse houses or better churches. The small glimpses we can gain of what Heckington was like in the years between 1500 and 1700 all agree that a few people lived in some style, while most others were pitifully poor.

The church dominated the physical environment, then as now. But a traveller back in time to the reign of the first Queen Elizabeth would be shocked to see that it was in a state of considerable disrepair. It had a badly leaking roof, which was flat rather than the pitched one we have now.

An early woodblock of the Church viewed from the southeast in the days when it still had a flat roof.
The restoration to what we have now began in 1867.

We know that in 1593 the whole of this roof had to be replaced and covered at great expense in new lead, which could be kept watertight and in good repair. Bell ringers must have been active even in those days, since the Vestry took the trouble to raise yet more money so that at least three bells could be taken down for repair, one being sent away to be recast in Nottingham. The present fourth and sixth bells were cast by George Oldfield in 1651 and 1633 respectively. Other bells would have been cast in or near the church itself. Large-scale repairs were also needed to the windows and new paving was laid inside the church. When the work was completed the Vestry paid various tradesmen ten shillings (50p) a year to maintain the new windows and eight shillings and four pence (about 42p) to keep the bells, ropes, frames and clappers in good repair. It is staggering to think that, even at the time of the Spanish Armada, St Andrew's was an old building, which the Vestry was struggling to preserve for people like us, four hundred years and more into the future.

What did the inside of St Andrew's church look like after Henry VIII's Reformation of the 1530s? The symbols of the old religion were removed one by one. The Chantry Chapels, situated in the north and south transepts, were closed down. These were places where daily prayers and masses used to be said for the souls of departed parishioners who had left money for this purpose.

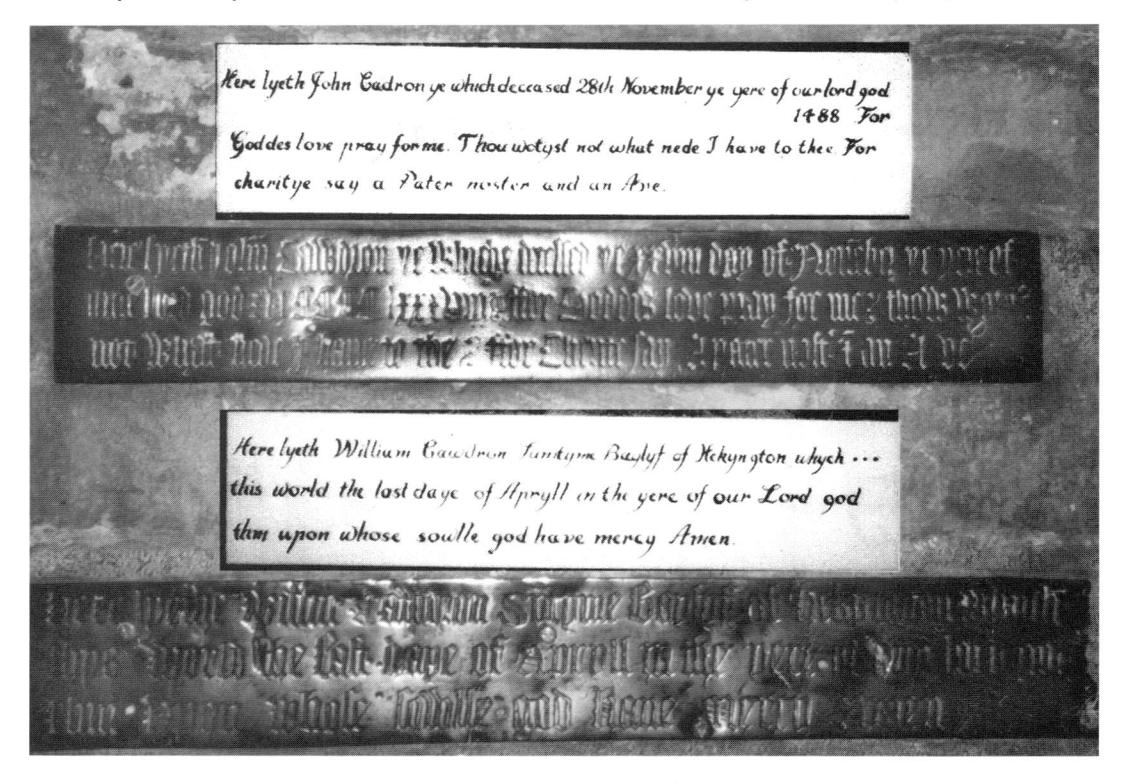

Plaques to the Cawdron family who left money for mass to be said.

But with the new Protestant faith, the altars were stripped and the Chantry priest pensioned off. From 1590 a new use was found for the south transept, formerly the Chantry of St Nicholas, as a burial place for the members of the important Christopher family from Winkhill Manor. It became known as the Winkhill Aisle and over thirty members of the Christopher family were eventually to be buried there.

Commonly known as the Winkhill Aisle, once the Chantry of the blessed Virgin Mary now the Lady Chapel. We can see the triple Sedilia set into the south wall. There is also a Piscina and Aumbry. The photograph is taken from the book "Saint Andrew's Church, Heckington" by Reverend D.C.Speedy BA.

At the start of Henry VIII's reign, the whole of the inside of the church would have been richly furnished and colourfully painted with plenty of gold leaf to catch the glow of the candle light. An imposing rood screen would have divided the Nave from the chancel, with a gallery stretching between the two high doors that can still be seen beyond the crossing, approached by turret staircases. In the chancel, the Easter Sepulchre, the Sedilia, the double-piscina and the tomb of Richard de Potesgrave would all have been brightly painted and gilded. Today only a few lines of this ancient decoration can be discerned above the vestry door. Most of the windows would have contained fine medieval stained glass. How soon after the Reformation were these walls, monuments and fittings stripped away? Some of the changes were certainly being made during the reign of Elizabeth I. The churchwardens' accounts for 1573 record money being paid out for *"washing the Easter wall in the chansell"*, which may well be a reference to the paint and gold leaf being whitewashed to cover them up in line with the plainer appearance of churches required by the Protestant faith. Nearly 25 years later we know that a new communion table and cloth were purchased to replace the *"Popish"* altar.

Although the wall paintings and decorations are almost illegible in Saint Andrew's at Heckington one survives at Saint Andrew's at Asgarby. In the register of listed buildings it is described as "a C15 wall painting of a kneeling robed figure with scrolled text on a deep red ground spangled with white flowers."
Photograph by Pat Banister.

We know that some of the medieval glass in the church windows was still in place in about 1640 when Gervase Holles, a local historian from Grimsby, visited St Andrew's to record the fittings. The two medieval founders of the church Richard de Potesgrave and Henry de Beaumont were both depicted in the stained glass, which is now sadly lost. We are fortunate, however, in still having a copy of the original 1300s image (copied in 1641) of Henry Beaumont with his wife, the former Lady Grantham. Other windows and memorials to Sir Henry de Asty and his wife may have been vandalised during the Civil War.

Sir Henry de Beaumont and his wife lady Grantham.

In medieval times there were many statues adorning the outside of the church as well as inside, standing on the niches in the walls. During the troubled times of the Reformation, the rise of Puritanism, the Civil War and Cromwell's Commonwealth, these exterior statues were removed and broken. Village tradition says that the pieces were built into the churchyard walls, but the puzzle for a modern passer-by is to wonder why just one medieval statue on the tower near the porch was allowed to remain and continues to stand in our own day.

The one remaining figure in the niche on the southwest corner of the Church tower is thought to represent Saint John by the carved eagle at the base.
Photographed by Kevin Teasdale.

At least after all the turmoil of the Civil War, Heckington seems to have regained a certain level of prosperity more quickly than some other parts of the country. With the Restoration of Charles II in 1660 there was much decay of towns and churches across the country. The parishioners of Heckington made what were then generous collections of between 23p and 42p for the aid of places such as "*Skarborow, for their dekaed church, 8/1, Milton, Dorset, 4/5, and Bridge North, Salop, 5/4*". These donations are listed on a leaf between the Baptisms and Burials in the first Parish Register. One wonders how many of these places had been heard of by the majority of the villagers, but at least in its church dealings Heckington was not an insular place.

THE TITHE BARN

Richard de Potesgrave was the last rector of Heckington having the right of receiving a portion of the villagers' agricultural produce as a tax or *tithe*. Bardney Abbey gained control of the church (and the tithes!) in 1345, which it kept until Henry VIII dissolved Bardney in 1536. From 1345 Heckington was served by a vicar who received a small salary or stipend and a small amount of land. The tithes of wheat, barley, rye, oats, peas and hay would have been collected by special agents and stored near the church in a tithe barn before being transported to Bardney. We know that there was such a barn in Heckington as, in 1575, some years after Bardney lost the use of it, the churchwardens' accounts tell us that the church *Laythe* (or barn) was re-thatched. If you walk down St Andrews Street you can catch a glimpse of a stone house behind a high wall. This was converted into a modern dwelling around 1980 from an ancient stone house that was once thatched and contained the remains of stone mullioned windows. Can it be that Heckington's medieval tithe barn was converted into that house and some of it still remains today behind that high wall?

Photograph of the old 'Tithe Barn' house off Saint Andrews Street taken at the end of the 19th century by M.C.Sumners. The blocked central door and massive central chimney stack are signs of a previous 'life.'

HOUSES OF THE RICH

After the death of Oliver Cromwell, King Charles II returned to England in 1660 to great rejoicing. However, this may have been short lived since the Restoration also led to the imposition of a Hearth Tax. This was paid by all but the poorest people and the tax increased depending on the number of fireplaces you had in your home. It is just typical that even though almost all the 1660s houses in Heckington have now disappeared, their tax returns have outlasted them and survived in the records. Taken along with other documents such as wills and the inventories of the contents of houses that were made when someone died, these records mean that we can begin to reconstruct the way of life of at least some of the wealthier inhabitants of the village.

In Tudor and Stuart times there were four manor houses associated with the village, each of which had six fireplaces indicating they were large buildings and home to wealthy people who could afford to pay a substantial Hearth Tax. They were Cobham Hall, which stood south of where the railway now runs beyond what is now Banks Lane, Winkhill Manor, north-east of the village towards the Fen, Holmes House, in the Fen at Garwick and the Manor at the north end of Church Street. It is a curious reminder of the continuity of history that all four great houses stood on land that we know was occupied from long before. Cobham Hall stood close to the site of a Roman villa and pieces of Roman tile can still be found mixed on the surface of the field with stone remnants of the Hall. Holmes House was on high ground in the fen since *'holme'* in Danish means land surrounded by water or marsh. In other parts of the county the name has been found associated with saltern mounds and so may link back to salt making in Heckington in Roman or even pre-Roman times. The third manor, Winkhill, is also known to be close to the site of a Roman building, again suggesting a long history of occupation. The fourth we deal with separately.

COBHAM HALL

Cobham Hall was also known as Heckington Hall and was the house of the lords of the manor of Heckington. Following the death of the last of the Beaumont clan around 1508, the manor passed through various branches of the de Broke family, some members of which used the title of Cobham. So in 1643, during the English Civil War, Sir John Broke, confusingly also known as Sir John Cobham, inherited the hall and estates. He seems to have been a major cattle and sheep farmer who made full use of his rights to grazing on the still existing common fields of the village. In fact he so overstocked the common land in Heckington Fen that the parishioners eventually did a deal with him. He agreed not to graze his animals on the common land and in return was awarded 600 acres of land all to himself to the east of the parish. This is the land beyond East Heckington still known as the Six Hundreds.

The old Cobham Hall was demolished sometime during the 18th century, though the stables and other buildings remained near an old fishpond until the 1790s. We can get a glimpse of what the Hall was like from an inventory of the rooms and their contents taken in 1707. The main ground floor rooms of the house were the hall, parlour, kitchen, dairies and pantries. The hall was furnished with two tables, thirteen chairs, and a quantity of pewter plates, tankards, brass pots and pans. Next to it, the parlour contained a four-poster bed as well as a long table, six leather chairs, two long forms, chests and a cupboard. This was a very old-fashioned way of living going back to medieval times where everyone would dine together at the two long tables in the main hall, while the best bed was next door in the parlour so the lord and lady could retire to sleep off their meal. In contrast to these arrangements in Heckington, neighbouring Howell Hall seems to have been much more advanced since we know that as early as 1633 Thomas Cheney had a separate dining parlour for himself and his family.

This leadwork, still in the Church bears the names of Henry Farrar and William Taylor, Churchwardens in 1681. Henry Farrar lived in Cobham Hall in 1707.
Photograph by Sandra Sardeson.

Returning to Cobham Hall, we know that on the first floor there were several bedrooms. One was the chamber over the hall, which contained a four-poster bed, another was known as the lodging chamber with two curtained beds (to keep out the draughts), and the third was a chamber over the kitchen with a bed, tub and other things, probably used as servants' quarters. What seems very odd to us now is that on the next floor above they used the four garret rooms for storing oats, beans, wheat and other things, presumably to keep them dry and away from mice. The contents of Cobham Hall and farm were valued in 1704 at £925, which was a great deal of money for those days.

HOLMES HOUSE

Holmes House stood on the east bank of the Car Dyke close to the hamlet of Garwick, approached from the road to Swineshead by a track which is still called Sandy Leas, now diverted to join the Fen Road. The best description we have of the old house comes from the Reverend George Oliver who reported that: *"Holmes House... was erected on a foundation of wrought stone, which reached to about three feet above the ground; the upper part of the edifice being composed of timber cross beams, filled in with mud and plaister. Its height was three stories. The front door was thickly set with nail heads, and had a curious ring or handle. The window frames, and indeed the whole of the timbers were very ancient and of oak."* When the house was demolished in 1810 a breast plate and back-piece of steel, and a curious coat-of-arms cast in clay were found inside. In the 1660s and 1670s Stephen Wiles, gentleman, and his wife Winifred, lived at Holmes House with their young family.

WINKHILL MANOR

The third stone-built manor house with six hearths was Winkhill, half a mile northeast of the village, the home of the Christopher family for nearly four hundred years from the 1580s.

The Christopher family coat-of-arms, A version of these arms, carved in stone and surrounded by a wreath of oak leaves was built into the front of at least two previous rebuildings of the house at Winkhill.

A moated medieval manor house stood on this site, to be replaced by several rebuildings over the years. The Christopher family may have rebuilt the house around 1638, since carved, dated stones survive from that time. This house had a spacious porch in front with a room above it. Over the door was a carved shield bearing the family arms. When the house was rebuilt again in 1780 these arms were re-inserted into the brickwork.

We get a glimpse of the seventeenth century house from George Christopher's inventory taken in 1668. The extensive rooms included the hall, kitchen, parlour, chamber over the parlour, the porch chamber, the Grantham chamber, the hall chamber, the chamber over the kitchen and dairies and brewhouse. The kitchen chamber was used for storing wheat and barley *"with other lumber there"*. The name *Grantham chamber* recalls a link back to the wife of Henry Beaumont, one of the founders of the church. We know that Thomas Grantham, gentleman, lived in Heckington from at least 1591 until his death in 1603. In his will, he asked to be buried in the church *"at my deske end and it for to be coffened"*.

HECKINGTON MANOR HOUSE

The fourth house having six hearths in the seventeenth century was the home of Mr Robert Taylor. this house was on the site of Heckington Manor, now the Ferdowse Clinic at the bottom of Church Street.

We have been able to trace the history of this site from earliest times to the present day. Originally called Boston Garth and the home of the Boston (or St Botolph) family who were important citizens (and vicars) in the 1200s and 1300s.

In the Subsidy rolls of 1332 Cedo de Sancto Botolfo (or Boston) paid 11s 4d, the second highest amount after Lady Isabel de Vesci, sister of Henry de Beaumont, Lord of the Manor.

A relic of this time remains in the name Fishpond lane, from Cowgate to the Playing field, which ran alongside a fishpond belonging to the medieval manor house.

The Cawdron family may have been the next occupiers of the site in the 1400s and 1500s. John Cawdron was buried in the Church in 1488 and William Cawdron "one time bailiff of Heckington" in 1544. His daughter married Robert Carre of Sleaford who bought up vast estates in the surrounding villages. In 1578 the Mansion House called Boston Garth was leased to William Taylor, whose family grew in wealth and importance in Heckington over the next 200 years. In 1665 Robert Taylor was living there, in a house that had two parlours, a Hall and three chambers, all with fire-places as well as a kitchen, dairy etc. His property was valued at £197 16s in 1676, but his descendant Anthony Taylor had property to the value of £2200 when he died in 1713, a vast amount of money in those days.

When the last male member of the Taylor family died the house and lands passed to the Godson family who lived at Heckington Manor from the late 1700s to around 1950. Earnest H Godson, who founded the firm of Solicitors in Sleaford, enlarged and altered the house in 1905 to how we see it today.

The house was bought by the County Council and became a Children's Home, then a Residential Home for the Elderly before being sold again to become the Ferdowse Clinic of today.

A carved stone showing the date 1632 from a rebuilding of the house at Winkhill in the reign of Charles I.
Photograph by Sandra Sardeson.

THE HOUSES OF THE POOR

There seems to have been quite a gulf between the way the rich and poor lived in the village in Tudor and Stuart times and among the poor we should perhaps include the vicar! It is true that the Vicarage had four hearths recorded in 1665, when Robert Thorpe was vicar. We might have expected the Vicarage to be next to the Church as now, but in the seventeenth century it was all of four miles away, on the road to South Kyme from the Boston Road where Glebe Farm still stands. This same vicarage was recorded In 1605 as consisting of *"foure bayes build all earthen walles covered with thatch, foure bayes being chambered with earth"*. So the vicar, like most of his parishioners, lived in a mud and stud dwelling, with the added inconvenience of a long walk or ride into the village. In 1671 we are told that the house contained *"one Hall and a Parlor with chambers over them, and two low Roomes with chambers over, one kitchen containing in all about four bays"*.

By contrast even to the Vicarage, the majority of the villagers lived in much poorer dwellings. Typical was William Gray who lived in Heckington Fenside, north of Holmes House. He was a labourer with a wife and six children when he died in 1689, leaving ten shillings (50p) to his eldest son, Edward, and one pound to each of his other children when they reached twenty-one. He also left one folding bed, one chest and one brass pot to his daughter Ann as her inheritance. There were people even poorer than the Gray family, however. In 1693 the elected overseers of the poor met and agreed on the fate of the village poor children. Widow Hayes was to keep Mary Petchell for £1, William Burton to keep Ann Clifton for £1 15s (£1.75p) and a pair of new shoes, and Widow Chapman was to receive £1 5s (£1.25p) for Robert Chapman. When Widow Patman died her goods were sold and the income used by the overseers to pay Benjamin Vincent towards the upkeep of her children Michael and Thomas. The Overseers were not so considerate to those they considered did not belong to the parish. We find in 1686 *"John Herrin and Katherin Herrin and one child, and Jonas Hay and wife and two children, and Barbary Peay and*

Eliz Nuball were openly whipped, at Heckington, the 28th day of May, and had a passe then made to convey them from constable to constable to Newark, in Nottinghamshire, and Will Stagg was at the same time whipped and sent to Nottinghamshire".

An image of Cowgate as it must have looked in medieval times. Original photograph taken in the early 1860s by M.C.Sumners. Digitally modified 2001 by P.Banister.

THE LAND

Heckington is a huge parish with over 5000 acres of land. As well as the open arable fields, the parish of the 1600s contained 2,330 acres of reasonably good grazing in the Fen, two-thirds of which was worth ten shillings (50p) an acre in 1633 and the wetter third was worth five shillings (25p) an acre. We can be absolutely certain that there were more animals than people living in Heckington. In 1563 the diocesan return records that there were 107 families in the village and we can assume an average of 4-5 people per family, giving a population of 4-500 people. Almost every family will have kept a pig and the richer ones will have had oxen or even horses for farm work. But the right to graze on the common land was used to the full by those who could afford to build up their stock of cattle and sheep. We have already noted that Sir John Broke so overstocked the Fen in 1633 that the parish gave him 600 acres of fenced land to keep his animals off the common fields. We also know that Lady Lockton of Swineshead had the right to graze 256 beasts and horses in Heckington Fen from May Day to Michaelmas, and the people of Burton Pedwardine had pasture rights in Heckington Fen in return for one day's labour. Mary Jenkinson who lived in Heckington at the end of Queen Elizabeth's reign admitted to keeping sixty cows, eight oxen, thirty horses, twenty young beasts and a thousand sheep in the fen!

In 1637 an attempt was made to enclose the remaining 1730 acres of common in the Fen. In spite of opposition from forty of the smallest landowners, the commissioners decided that it was in the best interests of the parishioners and one acre of Fen was to be allotted for each acre of arable land held, five acres was to be allocated for every cottage and toftstead, and the cottagers were to have their new land laid out as near to the town as possible. However it appears that this early enclosure scheme did not get very far, since records suggest that only a very small number of fields were enclosed near to the village before 1765. Because of this the Fen continued to be a place crowded with livestock for many years more.

Overall, Heckington in Tudor and Stuart times was a village of contrasts. Some wealthy people had thousands of pounds to their name, huge flocks of sheep in the fields and large manor houses to live in, even if their style of living was rather old-fashioned. For the majority of people houses were spread along much of the six-mile length of the parish. There were communities around Winkhill, at Garwick and East Heckington, near Holmes House, at Fenside north of Garwick, in Star Fen and to the west of the village around the group of windmills on the ridge towards Sleaford and Burton Pedwardine. Farms were amongst cottages throughout the village and not just relegated to the edges. Indeed there were farms close to the church until the 1960s. The appearance of the village was also different. The modern village is mostly red brick, but in King Charles II's day most of the houses would have been painted white, with lime mixed with animal fat to keep the rain out. It must have presented a postcard profile of white thatched cottages on a skyline dominated by the great stone Church.

CHAPTER FOUR

1700 - 1850: FROM A WATERY WORLD TO A MODERN WORLD

The period from 1700 to 1850 saw Heckington transformed from a village its medieval citizens would have recognised into a thriving community we can recognise today. At the beginning of the 18th Century the landscape was in many ways as the Romans had left it, with nearly half the parish little more than wasteland prone to constant flooding. In the village itself with a few solitary exceptions people's houses were still mud or clay walls under thatched roofs. The way of life was almost subsistence with people making a living out of what they could grow. Life was focused on the task of providing enough daily bread from strips of land in the common fields. Others, particularly in the Fen, lived by what they could gather from the water including fish and particularly wildfowl, geese were also kept in large numbers, not just for the meat but also for the regular crops of feathers that were plucked from the live birds. Indeed this was the origin of Fogartys and the whole Boston feather industry. Willows and osiers were used for making baskets and fencing. Reeds were harvested for thatching providing the best quality roofing.

> *The toiling Fisher here is tewing of his net*
> *The Fowler is imployd his lymed twigs to set*
> *One underneath his horse to get a shoot doth stalke*
> *Another over Dykes upon his stilts doth walke*
> *Ahere other with their spades, the Peats are squaring*
> *And others from Carres are busily about,*
> *To draw out Sedge and Reed for Thatch and Stover fit.*
>
> M Drayton, 1622

THE DECOY

Part of the harvest from the undrained fens was wild ducks, which were caught, killed and sent to market. They were shot or sometimes caught during the moulting season by using two boats with a net stretched between them. However a more efficient way of catching them, particularly as the wet areas decreased, was to use a *'decoy.'* It name derives from the Dutch word *'fendekooy,'* meaning a duck cage or trap. It consisted of narrow channels leading off a pond of around 3 acres, covered with hooped nets. The channels were curved and on the outside of the curves were screens made of rush mats. The decoy was worked by a decoyman, who first tamed a small group of ducks by feeding them regularly. These tame ducks or decoys attracted other wild ducks. The decoyman would sprinkle corn on the water in front of one of the channels. He would then introduce his trained dog into the water, which the ducks would chase, since they were emboldened by being in a large group. The decoyman, hiding behind the reed screens, patiently waited while the dog led the ducks towards him. The channels tapered down from around 18 feet at the entrance to only 18 inches at the tip. Once there, the net was dropped and the birds were caught and their necks wrung. It was not unusual for fifty or sixty wild ducks to be caught in such a drive.

1962.—Wild Duck Decoy, Lincolnshire.

Heckington's decoy is shown on a drainage survey map of 1804. It was at the eastern edge of the parish on the Six Hundreds Farm. The 18th century fenland poet, William Hall, worked there for some time. He records that, *"The pond about 3 acres of water, well-sheltered and distant from disturbance, became so great an asylum that I have heard divers decoymen say it was apparently impossible for an egg to drop without hitting another duck. Our house was a full mile distant but when the birds were disturbed any stranger would suppose it distant thunder - 'From raised decoy these ducks on flight, By tens of thousands darken light' "*.

DICK TURPIN

The common lands were used by all the villagers for grazing their animals. Lincolnshire was also a centre for horse breeding. It was from one of Heckington's open fields that the highwayman Dick Turpin stole the horses that led to his downfall and execution. He travelled regularly from his home at Long Sutton (under a false name of Palmer) along what is now the A17 up to Yorkshire and was a regular customer at the village inns in Heckington.

On one of his journeys in 1738 he stole two horses belonging to Thomas Creasey of Heckington, which were grazing in the common village open fields. Amazingly Turpin then spent the night undetected at his Heckington haunt. Next day he took the horses up to Yorkshire and tried unsuccessfully to sell them. He must have been a hothead as he had an argument with someone and was arrested for a brawl, which included his shooting a cockerel in the street! While under arrest for this petty crime, one of Thomas Creasey's fellow villagers passed through Beverley and recognised the two horses as those stolen from Creasey. Fate dealt Turpin another cruel blow when he wrote to his brother for help. While the letter was awaiting collection in his home village, his former schoolmaster identified it as Turpin's handwriting. Turpin might have escaped the brawling charge with a minor sentence, but he was convicted of stealing Creasey's horses and as horse stealing was a capital offence he was hanged at York on 7th April 1739.

Born in 1705 at the Bell Inn, Hempstead, Essex, Dick Turpin was apprenticed to a butcher at the age of 16 in London. He later married and set up in business on his own. In 1729 he was caught selling stolen meat and went on the run. He eventually became a highwayman and the rest as they say is history.

DRAINAGE

So what happened to change this watery, lawless world? Since Roman times people had realised that the productivity of the soil could be increased if only it could be drained and protected from the constant flooding that had affected the fenland from time immemorial. Conditions in Heckington are recorded in a poem by William Hall, known as Low Fen Bill, who lived at Five Willow Wath on the boundary between the South Kyme and Heckington fens.

> *Near the Garrick milestone*
> *Nothing there grew beneath the sky*
> *But willows scarcely six feet high,*
> *Or osiers barely three feet dry,*
> *And those of only one year's crop*
> *The flood did fairly overtop.*
>
> William Hall (1748-1825)

The 18th Century was to see the first significant progress and success in Heckington since Roman times. Drainage projects elsewhere in Lincolnshire had shown the tremendous increase in the value of land and the excellent crops that it could produce. During the 1750s landowners in South Lincolnshire explored ways of draining their own lands and reaping the benefits it would bring. The two issues they had to get to grips with were raising the water into the river Witham and then improving the flow of the river itself so that the floodwater could be moved more quickly out to sea.

Finally in 1762 an Act of Parliament was granted for a major improvement scheme. This diverted the River Witham on a new straight course for approximately five miles to improve its flow. It also allowed construction in 1766 of the Grand Sluice at Boston. The purpose of this was to prevent tidal waters backing up the river and it can still be seen in operation today at the Sluice Bridge in Boston with its sluice gates that can be opened or closed depending on the state of tide and river. Pumps, looking like windmills, were also built at strategic places on the drains to lift water up into the river. Heckington had four pumping mills of its own, all situated at the north eastern edge of the parish where water from local drains was lifted up into the Head Dyke. The village field walking group can testify that the foundations and sluices for these now ruined mills still survive in the fen nearly 250 years after they were built. This work was to bring about important physical and economic changes to the village.

ENCLOSURE
The wild fenlands, which had hitherto been little more than rough grazing, were transformed by better drainage into profitable arable land. In some villages rents rose from 1/6d (7.5p) per acre to 11/- (55p) or even 17/- (85p) per acre, which were considerable sums in the 18th century. Drainage was a crucial step without which land improvement was impossible, but it was only a beginning. Further agricultural progress depended on re-dividing the common fields into efficient holdings and enclosing them with hedges. Only then could farmers apply the new machinery and methods of farming that were being invented. Once the drainage of the fens seemed certain with the passing of the drainage act in 1762, the Heckington landowners immediately began the task of enclosing the village fields and an act of Parliament for this purpose was obtained in 1763.

The Enclosure Act achieved two things. Firstly ownership of strips that had been scattered all over the six open fields of the parish was consolidated into single, cohesive holdings. Secondly the 2,250 acres of common land were divided up amongst landowners so that they could be farmed effectively. The new fields were enclosed by post and rail fences under planted with hedges, and hundreds of thousands of hawthorns were planted. Very quickly the landscape around the village changed from wide-open spaces punctuated by stands of alder and willow to the enclosed fields surrounded by hedgerows that we have come to regard as traditional.

> Enclosure of the open fens required a special Act of Parliament. A copy of the first page of the Heckington 'Inclosure Act' of 1763 is reproduced here.
> It begins by mentioning the six hundred acres of land previously put aside.

AN

A C T

FOR

Dividing and Inclosing the open Common Fields, Common Meadows, and other Commonable Lands in the Parish of *Heckington*, in the County of *Lincoln*.

Whereas the open Fields, Meadow Grounds, common Fen, Cow Pasture, and other commonable Places within the Parish of *Heckington*, in the County of *Lincoln*, are computed to contain Four thousand Acres, or thereabouts:

And whereas Lady *Fraiser* is Lady of the Manor and Patroness of the Vicarage of *Heckington* aforesaid, but has no Property in the said open Fields or Meadow Grounds; and in lieu of Six hundred Acres severed from the said common Fen of *Heckington* aforesaid, called or known by the Name of the *Six Hundreds*, and now in the Possession of the said Lady *Fraiser*, has no Right or Interest in the said common Fen, Cow Pasture, or other commonable Places of *Heckington* aforesaid; *Anthony Taylor*, Esquire, is Impropriator of the Great Tythes arising, renewing, increasing, or happening within

Seventy-three owners were awarded land in 1764. Sixteen had large holdings, which amounted to over 70% of the enclosed land, while the remaining 30% was shared among the rest. Enclosure was an expensive business. Not only did the land itself have to be enclosed, but obtaining an act of Parliament and administration all had to be paid for. The Heckington Enclosure cost the enormous sum of £3,636. These costs were shared amongst the owners in proportion to the land they received. In some villages the costs were so great that smaller owners had to sell most of their land to meet their share of the expenses. However, in Heckington at least, it seems that most landowners were able to retain their holdings. The land in the fen was re-surveyed in 1804 in connection with improvements to the drainage and it has been possible to compare the ownership of each field forty years after the enclosure in 1765. Very little had changed hands, so the enclosure seems to have benefited the village overall.

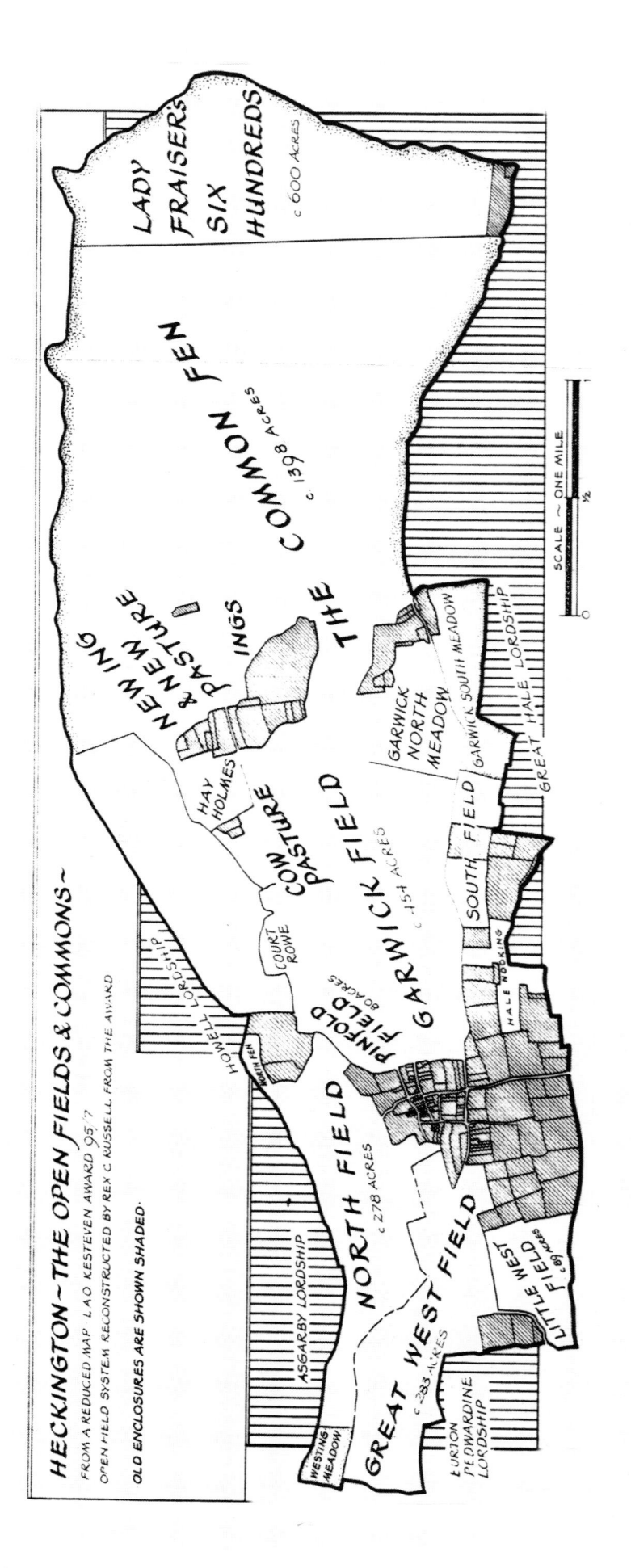

Heckington parish map before the inclosure of 1764 by permission of and reconstructed from the Award by Rex Russell.

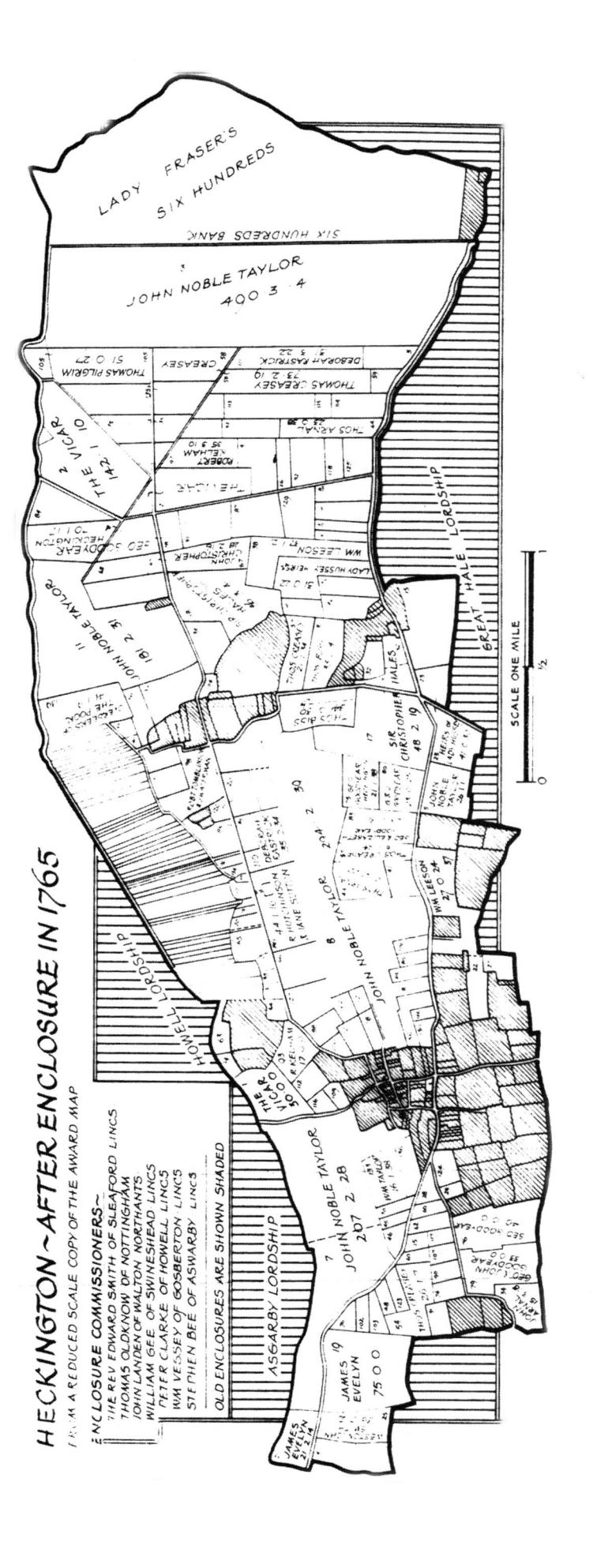

Map of Heckington parish after the inclosures of 1764 by permission of and reconstructed from the award by Rex Russell.

Enclosure did, however, mark the end of the medieval landscape. The large open fields were divided into smaller ones surrounded by the hedges of hawthorn, blackthorn, field maple and elder that we take for granted today. The old system of strip farming disappeared. The over-grazing of the common fields had disappeared, with landowners now being obliged to limit their flocks to the amount of grazing land they actually owned.

HEDGES IN MODERN TIMES

Although we think of hedge lined fields as an established part of the Lincolnshire countryside, more than 50% of the field hedges in the parish have disappeared in recent years and you would not need a computer to be able to count all the ones that are left. Hedges are interesting because they tell us things about the layout of the fields and roads in the past. It is even possible to roughly date hedges. This is done by counting the number of woody species in a 30-metre length. Every new species encountered adds approximately 100 years to the age of the hedge. Unfortunately the counting can be affected by modern planting so it very important to keep formal records as people soon forget what was planted and when.

As well as counting species, another clue to an old hedge is the presence of dogwood, field maple or spindle amongst the planting, since these were favoured even before the enclosures of the 18th century. The Heckington fieldwalking group takes a break in the summer and exchanges muddy fields for hedge surveying. Our survey has found plenty of hawthorns, including the midlands hawthorn, which is more commonly a woodland species. In addition there is plenty of blackthorn for making sloe gin, elder for elderberry wine, and wild roses for their beauty in the summer. We know some of the hedges are over 500 years old, for example a short stretch of hedge on the left of the A17 towards Boston soon after the end of the bypass.

However, not all the changes in the landscape are due to human action. One of the most recent changes is due to Dutch Elm disease, which in the 1970s ravaged the graceful elm trees that were such a feature of John Constable's landscape paintings. Careful survey has identified many ancient tree stumps in hedgerows that seem to be elm. But it should not be thought that the elms are all dead. They live on in large numbers in the hedgerows and only seem to succumb to the disease if they are allowed to grow up from the hedge to form trees. The far end of the hedge beside the footpath at the end of Cameron Street has some upwardly mobile elms still untouched, so there may be hope that the elm is finally beginning to develop some resistance to the ravages of the disease.

Part of a Heckington hedgerow showing a regrowing elm on the right and with the parish Church in the distance.
Photographed by Kevin Teasdale.

HOUSES

The improvements in farming that resulted from draining and enclosing the parish brought a wave of prosperity unparalleled in Heckington history. A description of the village written in 1826 tells us of *"an unusual number of most excellent houses, that give an air of great respectability, wealth and comfort to this exceedingly cheerful village"*. This can still be seen in some of the houses in the village today. Many of Heckington's finest houses date from the years following the enclosure as prosperous landowners and farmers enjoyed their new found wealth.

LATE 18th AND EARLY 19th CENTURY HOUSES

* No 4 the Green (late 18C)
* The Red House, 63 High Street (1797)
* Albion House, 15 Church Street (1810)
* 103 High Street (1793)
* 42 High Street (1830)

Rebuilding was not confined to the grander houses. Some charming terraces were built, most of which were recently demolished to make way for modern development. Surviving individual buildings include:

* 67 and 69 Church Street (late 18th or early 19th century)
* 2 Church Street (1790)
* 18 Boston Road (1804)

At number 4 the Green we have a fine example of a red brick Flemish bond house with a pantiled roof and raised brick coped gables with brick gable stacks. Also of note is the plain front parapet and flat topped sash bay windows.
Photograph by Pat Banister.

The Red House. Built circa 1787 and in red brick Flemish bond with a slate roof and raised stone coped gables with 2 gable stacks. All the sash windows have flat rubbed brick arched heads. Another interesting feature is the cast iron railings at the front.
Photograph by Pat Banister 1999.

Number 103 High Street was built in 1793 and is red brick in flemish bond with a pantiled Mansard roof with raised brick coped gables and 2 gable stacks. It is single storey plus attics. The plain tiled porch with eliptical arch is a later addition.
Photograph by Sally Banister.

Number 15 Church Street has the patriotic name of Albion House. It is red brick flemish bond with a tiled roof and 2 gable stacks, sash windows and 2 flat roofed sash bays. There is also a fine six panel front door with mouldings.
Photograph by Sally Banister.

Investment was not just confined to houses. Until the end of the 18th century, the village's corn was ground by what the Enclosure Act referred to as "ancient windmills", which were probably post mills dating back to the Middle Ages. Three modern windmills on Sleaford Road replaced these in the 19th century. The tower of one of these still survives. The second stood on the site of Woodman's Park and was destroyed by fire in 1894. The third stood in the fields where Mayflower Drive now stands. Each of these probably cost more than £1,000 to build at a time when the weekly wage was less than 50p.

This splendid photograph shows the remaining mill on Sleaford road in all its glory and is dated 1935. Within twenty years it had deteriorated into an abandoned shell.

ROADS

The roads were certainly in need of improvement before this time, being made up of nothing much more than small stones or gravel. In 1759 John Cowley, the parish surveyor, reported on the road from Heckington to Great Hale. The road was wide - up to 37 feet in places - but very deeply rutted. The ruts were in places one foot nine inches and even two feet deep! The road must have been virtually impassable when Cowley took his measurements in the depths of winter on 6th January.

Communications were improved later that year when the main road through the village was taken over by the Lincoln Heath and Market Deeping Turnpike Trust. This meant that road users now had to pay a toll to the Trust, which was then obliged to maintain and improve the road. Toll bars were set up at junctions including Side Bar Lane between Garwick and East Heckington. Initially the turnpike road linked Sleaford and Boston. It was not until 1826 that the road from Swineshead to Kings Lynn was similarly improved, although a stagecoach service, which passed through the village on its way from Newark to Kings Lynn, called in for a regular stop at the Royal Oak on the High Street.

Sleaford Road before it was paved. Road maintenance was paid for by the parish and carried out by lengthsmen. Each being responsible for a given 'length' of road and often having to smash the stone to a workable size with a hammer before it could be used. This would be tipped on the roadside at convenient intervals by horse and cart after collection from the railway station.
Photograph by M.C.Sumners.

Water was also used as a form of transport. The Parish Registers record at least two boatmen living in the village in the second half of the 18th century. They would have used the drains and the river Slea that had been improved for navigation in 1792. They would also have come into their own during the winter flooding, which continued to some extent despite the improved drainage. The design of Boston's Grand Sluice caused it to silt up regularly and sometimes lack of wind at wet times meant that the pumping mills were unable to operate. It is recorded that Heckington Fen flooded every winter between 1795 and 1801 and in very cold weather the fenland even froze so hard that it was said to be possible to skate from the village all the way to Boston. The winter flooding was only overcome in the 1820s when the wind-driven pumps were finally replaced by steam pumps that could operate independent of the weather.

A CHANGING SOCIETY
Without modern facilities for travel, parish affairs were almost all handled at local level. Most matters were dealt with by the Parish Vestry, who were responsible for the care of the poor, the maintenance of the roads and policing of the streets. They elected individuals to discharge these duties - the overseers of the poor, the surveyor of the highways, and the parish constable. The Enclosure Act of 1764 also made the Vestry responsible for maintaining the drainage mills in the Fen, so each year a village worthy would receive the grand title of *'Engine Master.'*

Following the disruption to poor relief caused by the dissolution of the monasteries, the Poor Law Act of 1601 eventually established a new system of providing for the poor. It was funded by a parish rate. The system was that the parish provided the poor and elderly with a basic minimum standard of living, but expected them to work in return. Sometimes widows were paid to care for orphaned or destitute children, very neatly resolving two problems at once.

Constable Swinney of Heckington photographed in 1848. Although from the M.C.Sumners photographs we can't be sure if it was taken by him. At this time it is certainly the oldest known photograph of anyone connected with the village and quite possibly one of the oldest photographs of a policeman.

Larger and more organised parishes such as Heckington also ran special buildings called workhouses. Some were purpose built; others were simply in existing cottages. A government survey in 1776 showed Heckington as having a workhouse. This had been in existence for some years as the vestry accounts record that it was re-thatched by John Hepton for 11/4d (57p) in 1768 only to be burned down and replaced in 1813. The new building had a relatively short life as a workhouse but survives today as White Horse House on Church Street. The 1834 Poor Law Amendment Act saw parishes being grouped together, and Heckington became part of the Sleaford Union in 1836. A large new workhouse was built at Sleaford, and the Heckington workhouse was sold in 1837.

If you stand in front of the old White Horse and look up and to the left of the front door you will see this commemorative stone.
Photographed by C.Pinchbeck 2001.

The vestry accounts also tell us of the basic workhouse diet of potatoes and hog's lard. Parish provision meant that one was unlikely to starve, although there was some shame attached to being on the Parish and this was a deliberate encouragement to thrift and self-reliance. As early as 1748, a Friendly Society was formed in Heckington. Members paid regular subscriptions and this formed a fund to make payments when members were ill or infirm. The society continued its existence until around 1940, by which time the insurance companies and later the welfare state took over. The need for local provision fell away, although with it was lost some of the sense of moral and social purpose built up through mutual welfare provision with one's neighbours.

RELIGIOUS LIFE

After the religious turmoil of the Reformation and Civil War, the 18th century was notable for two things, the decline of the established church, and increasing tolerance of non-conformity, which had first shown itself in the Toleration Act of 1689. Both a symptom and a cause of the wane of the established church was the practice of absentee vicars. They collected the parish revenue but lived elsewhere and made no contribution to the spiritual or pastoral needs of their parishes. Heckington was a victim of this trend. The vicar of 1712, Thomas Townsend, is recorded as having the Bishop of Lincoln's permission to live at Court in London. Into this vacuum came John Wesley and the Methodists who offered a highly organised, very personal form of Christianity. Non-conformity was often particularly strong in villages such as Heckington, where there was no controlling, Anglican, landowner to offer discouragement. It is said that by 1790, half the population of Heckington called itself Methodist.

The first written records of a dissenting congregation relates to the Particular Baptists in 1772. Seven men and their ministers met at Garwick in the house of John Whitehead, perhaps a descendant of the John Whitehead who kept Dick Turpin's pub. After moving around members' houses, they built a permanent chapel in Eastgate by 1802. This remained in existence until 1978.

The Methodists had a chapel by 1809, which belonged to William Lee. A new building was erected in 1835 in St Andrew's Street. Replaced in 1905 by the building in Church Street, the old chapel still survives as Church House. The 1835 building seated 290, with additional accommodation for 150 Sunday school children.

The old Methodist chapel as it is today. Now known as Church House it has been a public reading room and a polling station. It is now used for meetings and children's play groups. Photographed by Charles Pinchbeck 2001.

One of the Methodists' high points was the arrival of a special visiting preacher on 30th March 1851, the day of the Religious Census. The period saw much recrimination and division in the Methodist movement nationally. The first split was in 1810, when the Primitive Methodists seceded from the main body. There was a Primitive Methodist presence in Heckington by 1821, when one of the itinerant preachers, William Fieldsend, visited the village and *"found them not in such a flourishing state as expected"*. In 1832 one of their number, George Bee, a Peninsular War veteran, adapted a barn in the Fen for their use. In 1855, a purpose-built chapel was erected on Side Bar Lane. This was financed by the Minkley family, who had moved into the village from Nottinghamshire from about 1850 onwards. Rebuilt in 1873, it finally closed its doors in 1970, and was converted into a house.

Fen chapel Side bar Lane now a private house. Photographed in 2000 by Pat Banister.

Yet another split occurred in 1850 when the Wesleyan Reform group seceded from the main Church in response to a nationwide desire for greater lay involvement in the Church. This national division had clear local implications. Four Methodist preachers based in Heckington all resigned and joined the Wesleyan Reform Union. By 1852 they had built yet another chapel in what was then called South Street, now Eastgate. Towards the end of the period, the Anglican church began to re-establish itself. At the time there was a strong movement to encourage vicars to live in their parishes by building them decent houses. In Heckington's case a modern and commodious vicarage was built in 1822 on the Howell Road glebe land to replace the previous building in Heckington Fen. It was built by the new vicar, Reverend Henry Bristowe Benson, at his own expense.

The proverbial vicarage tea party in progress on the lawn in the late 1800s when the Howell Road vicarage was still being put to the use for which it was built.
It is now known as 'The Old Vicarage.'

VILLAGE LIVELIHOODS

Whilst there were no trade directories or census details on employment, the baptismal registers from the 1650s onwards give details of the father's occupation, enabling a useful picture to be built up of the working life of the village. Many cottagers or labourers supported themselves by working small plots of land, mixed with days of paid work on the larger farms. Others fall into two main groups. Firstly, there are the tradesmen who met the everyday needs of the village: the butcher and baker, the bricklayer and the carpenter. In addition, there was a wide range of tradesmen who made more important things that today would be mass-produced elsewhere, even abroad, and brought in. The bakers' flour would have been milled in the village, even by the baker himself. The Stamford Mercury of 1793 carried an advertisement for *"a youth between 15 - 16 years of age as an apprentice to ...... Thomas Arnold, Miller and Baker, Heckington"*. The bricklayer would have used bricks made by Samuel and William Banks, at Heckington's own brickyard in Star Fen. Most villagers would have worn clothes, shoes, even gloves made by village craftsmen.

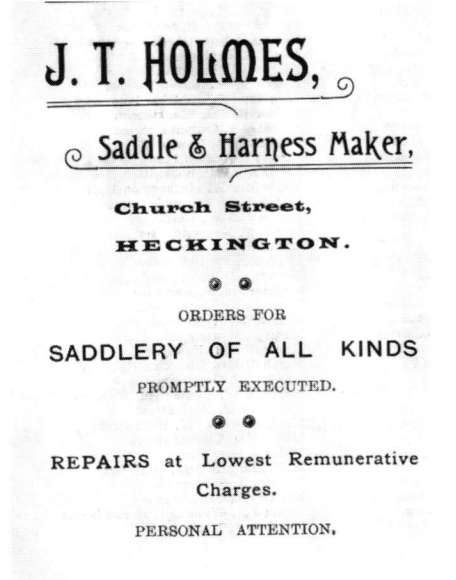

J. T. HOLMES,
Saddle & Harness Maker,
Church Street,
HECKINGTON.

ORDERS FOR
SADDLERY OF ALL KINDS
PROMPTLY EXECUTED.

REPAIRS at Lowest Remunerative Charges.
PERSONAL ATTENTION.

Copies of two handbill advertisements from local tradesmen of the period. C. Mowbray at one time owned the Sleaford Road mill.

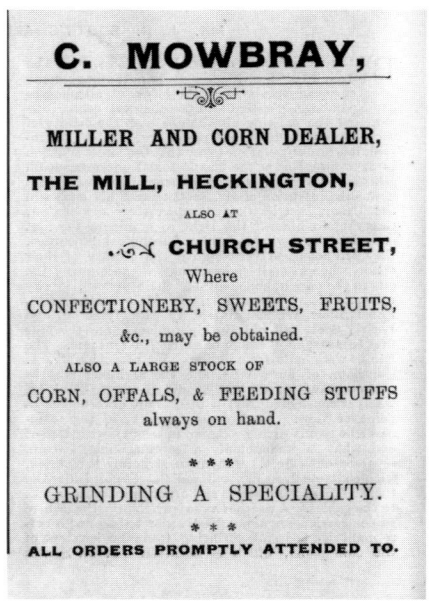

C. MOWBRAY,

MILLER AND CORN DEALER,
THE MILL, HECKINGTON,
ALSO AT
CHURCH STREET,
Where
CONFECTIONERY, SWEETS, FRUITS,
&c., may be obtained.
ALSO A LARGE STOCK OF
CORN, OFFALS, & FEEDING STUFFS
always on hand.

GRINDING A SPECIALITY.

ALL ORDERS PROMPTLY ATTENDED TO.

The main business of the parish - farming - also had most of its needs met in the village. Power for working the land was provided by horses, whose harnesses were made by saddlers and collar makers such as Joseph Hooper. The harvest was gathered in using wagons made by the village wheelwrights, Daniel Baxter, Samuel Lincoln and John Stanton. There were also some surprising occupations with the undrained fens supporting a fisherman, Edward Stalworth, and two boatmen, John Louton and Thomas Macklewain.

Leading sheaves to the stackyard at High Grounds farm in the days when the horse was the kingpin of the agricultural way of life. The stacks would be 'thacked' to keep out the rain and then threshed later in the year.

CONCLUSION

The eighteenth century saw increasing prosperity within the village as a result of the enclosing of the open fields and improvements in agriculture that followed. The village still remained self sufficient and enclosed from the outside world as it had in earlier times. Continuing economic growth in the nineteenth and twentieth centuries was to see living standards rise still further and the village come into wider contact and greater dependence on the outside world.

CHAPTER 5

Victorian Heckington 1850-1914

SOME TASTERS OF LIFE IN VICTORIAN HECKINGTON

With the coming of the Victorian era many more people were learning to read and write and new technologies were making the printing of newspapers and their distribution easy and comparatively cheap. Without television or radio people quite literally kept up with local and national news through the press. There were also more people who had some time in which to write letters and keep diaries. So for the first time in this story of Heckington we have a plethora of material in a time when every day life was changing increasingly rapidly. Because of this we have had to be very selective and can only give you a taster of everyday life and perhaps tempt you to learn more.

Heckington's population rose steadily during the first half of the century from 1,042 in 1820 to reach a peak of 1,865 in 1871, with a housing stock of 440 houses. At this time almost 84% of the population had been born within a 20-mile radius of the village and nearly 40% had been born within the village itself. The death rate among children was high, with nearly a quarter of all burials being children under five in the period 1870-1879. Even so, 40% of the population at this time is recorded as being less than 15 years of age as the nineteenth century drew to its close; there was a gradual decline in the population of the village until by 1901 it stood at 1901. Since then the numbers of people living in the village has grown with a very dramatic growth in the last few years of the 20th century so that it is now topping 3000 and still rising.

AGRICULTURE
The Economy of the Village
Farming remained the mainstay of life and livelihood that it had always been. An account of the farming year survives from that time: -

The Annual Round
January: a grim month when even the father himself would often be out of work. All that was available was hedging and ditching.
February: hoeing winter wheat, setting beans.
March dropping spring corn, gathering stones. Children in Heckington remember spending hours gathering stone from the fields to the West of the Car Dyke at Holmes House. They scared themselves with repeating legends of a mysterious great house, which had fallen down following some forgotten disaster. (Archaeological excavations in the 1960's proved this to be the site of the Roman tile kilns)
April /May: pulling up couch grass.
June: haymaking and hoeing.
July: singling turnips and beet
August/September: Harvest EWA 'Children made bands to bind sheaves up'
October: dibbling wheat, cutting turnips. Turnips had to be heaved out; a fork could not be used as it damaged the root. This work caused blisters on the children's hands.
November/December: ploughing, hedging, ditching or if no work no pay

As the century progressed so did farming and the life of the traditional farming community began to change radically. The twenty years from 1850 -1870 were boom years for British farming. During these years the progressive farmers in Heckington as elsewhere fertilised their land, fed their cattle with oilcake and cheap imported grain and were the first to use the new machinery being invented. We are fortunate to have contemporary views of two Heckington men with a different perspective on the farm mechanisation mentioned above:

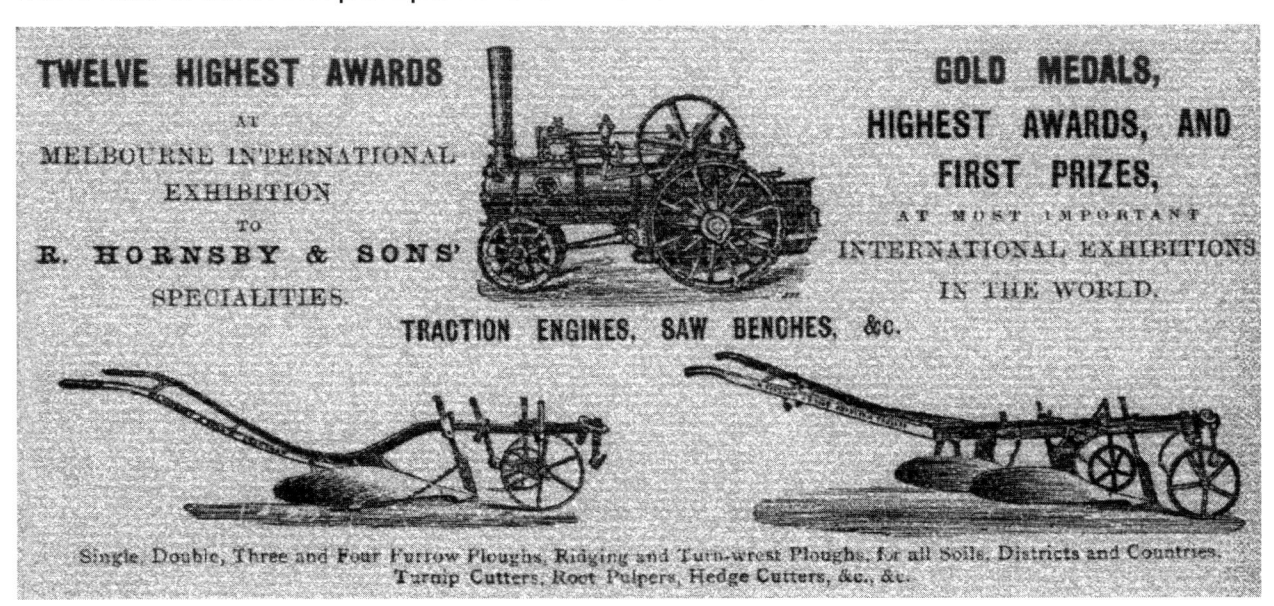

An early advertisement for agricultural machinery

William Little, who owned the Hall estate recorded on 31st July 1865 'Started reaping machine. The weather rather unsettled. This implement will be of great aid to the farmer and no injury to the respectable labourer. A meeting took place at the Royal Oak Inn to make arrangements about steam ploughing. W.Topper the general Manager and Mr Sharpe were present. The three Tomlinsons, G.Godson, R.Godson, J.Godson, C.H.Little and W.Little guaranteed the required number of acres. The Manager engaged that any member of our Society shall at all times have the implement by giving six days notice although it may be engaged for other parties.'

Harold Cook, son of the village blacksmith was less positive. 'Unfortunately the coming of the reaping machine reduced gleaning possibilities considerably by ousting the Irish harvesters, who came to the district in large numbers and used the traditional scythes and then at about the turn of the century there arrived the self-binder which left nothing to glean. I remember the first binder being used. It broke down and my ingenious father repaired it.'

The mighty steam engines used to power the threshing drums must have been an extreme fire hazard in those early days.

Then a series of wet seasons and the flooding in of cheap American wheat and frozen meat brought this prosperity crashing into ruins. After 1875 a catastrophic depression set in, the effects of which were to be felt long into the future with agriculture only really recovering with the second world war. In fact, this crisis was largely due to British inventions: railways, steam ships and refrigeration. The appalling weather conditions with continuous rain not only ruined crops but also created conditions for the spread of diseases such as; Rinderpest, foot and mouth and foot rot in sheep, to spread among the weakened animals. William Little wrote of this in his diary.

 As we have been pulling together the material for this book little did we imagine that a similar cattle plague would again hit the country. This time Lincolnshire escaped but William Little's sorrow rings down the centuries with a meaning with which we can now truly empathise.

12th March 1866: 'This dreadful cattle plague will be talked of by a future generation, but they will never realise what it is to go into a farm yard and you may see at this moment 20,30,40 head of stock all hanging up of all ages sizes and qualities under hovels in stables and anywhere space can be found.'

When the weather improved falling prices caused by the rapidly increasing import of food lead to further recession in British farming. Imports of wheat from North America and beef from Argentina were particularly significant. [At this time transport costs were the same from North America to England as Sleaford to Manchester for example a frozen lamb carcass cost only 1shilling to transport to England

Then in the early 1890's, particularly 1894 drought developed with the resultant loss of fodder; 'seed did not even germinate.' It was so dry there was nothing for cattle to eat. 'All the leaves were stripped from the trees as high as the cattle could reach'

In 1896 a Royal Commission was set up to enquire into the Causes of Agricultural Depression. In fact it was not so bad in Lincolnshire as in some other parts of the country because farmers had already begun to diversify in the way that the Commission's finding were to recommend.

However, in his evidence to the commission one Heckington tenant farmer with a holding of 186 acres arable and 120 acres pasture reported that: System of farming, breeding stock and fattening them for the market. All his buildings were in good condition, the drainage good and he had a good water supply, but the value of his farms had fallen from £985 per annum in 1882 to £450 in 1895.

Despite the onset of mechanisation farming at this time still required a great deal of labour. This was often provided by gangs of women and children. The House on Church Street facing Cameron Street was a tailor's shop. The Proprietor was also the chief gangmaster / surveyor in the village. He measured up and assessed the amount of work the gangs were to do. Women and children were needed for seasonal work and it was heavily relied upon as an essential part of the family income.

In 1843 and 1867 Royal Commissions were set up to enquire into the employment of women and children. The Gang System was prevalent and the work was exhausting, unhealthy and morally dangerous. Children had generally started work full time by the time they were 10. In Lincolnshire the wages for women were 10d a day, 1s for weeding and 2s at harvest time. The Commissioners were not in favour of employing girls because of the moral danger.

Toynbee who farmed rich grazing and fen land in Heckington is quoted as never employing women and children except in weeding time and then only employing girls of 15 & 16 with their mothers. He explained he made every endeavour to drive them into service. "It's a very bad thing keeping great girls at home with their parents: they generally come to no good"

A CHILD'S EYE VIEW OF GLEANING

To children of my day Harvest time meant long hours spent under a glorious blue sky, the sun beating down upon us and turning our limbs golden brown and our cheeks pink as only God's good fresh air can do.

It was a time of hard work for us also because we were "Gleaners". There were two or three gangs of "Gleaners" in the village at that time.

A scout would keep his eyes open for a field of corn almost ready for cutting and the news would spread around the members of that particular gang.

We would watch carefully as the corn was cut and then stooked and left ready to dry for several days and then at last the wagons and horses would start to gather up the sheaves of corn and take them away to be stacked and threshed at a later date.

It was the rule of the gleaners that whilst one stook of corn remained in the field we were "Honour bound" not to start gleaning because this meant that the field had not had its final racking. Once the field was empty it became a hive of activity. We would leave home by 7 o'clock in the morning. Even small mites of 5 or 6 years of age would walk with their mothers to Howell or the bottom of Heckington Fen. Quite often the mother would have a small baby in the pram and would have to feed it in the field and then go on gleaning.

On reaching the field we were given a small white calico bag, which we tied around our waist and into which we put our ears of corn. I am horrified now at the thought that we small children carried by our sides an open razor, which we used to cut off the haulms of the wheat before putting the ears into our bag. These small bags of corn, when full were transferred to a big sack, which we hoped to fill before the day's work was over.

We would glean all day apart from the two small breaks for sandwiches and a drink of cold tea or water, as this was before the invention of the Thermos flask. About 3p.m. We would start to pack our bags ready for the long trek home.

By the end of the summer holidays we had acquired sufficient corn to keep our chickens all through the winter. I think this was no mean achievement for small children to do with no hope of reward, but just a sense of satisfaction in helping the family exchequer.

Children gleaning in the fens. Photographed by F.Parkinson 1873-1956. Lincolnshire Museums.

HOME LIFE OF THE COTTAGER
The Domestic economy

It required considerable thrift and economy to raise a family on a labourer's wage. The following account of the domestic economy of the typical labouring family gives a vivid picture of making ends meet at the turn of the century. 'The economy of the village was based entirely on agriculture and all branches of farming. The Average weekly wage of nearly all the families was not more than ten shillings per week. Rents would be from two to four shillings per week: The rent of each of the terraced houses in St Andrew's Street was four shillings per week inclusive of rates. The owner was D.G. Harris, who had the printing works virtually opposite in the grounds of St Andrew's Villa, which was his home. Fresh meat was purchased once a week, when it could be afforded and for this and the week's meagre groceries payment was mostly made one week in arrears. But all this did not by any means mean poor living. Most of the cottagers fed one or two pigs and the resulting bacon and hams became the mainstay for food for the greater part of the year. Killing the pig and getting it 'out of the way' was a time of great activity, excitement and plenty, with the attendant pork pies, sausages, scraps and other delicacies.

Many people kept chickens and from time to time there were eggs for sale to augment the family income. Also the occasional chicken and rabbit went to the pot. Nobody bought vegetables: - potatoes, carrots, turnips, parsnips were graved down for the winter and the method of preserving eggs in lime was largely used. Gleaning by the many children in the village had an important effect on the economy and large families would gather enough ears of corn, which when threshed and then ground at the mill augmented the swill and boiled potatoes given to the pigs. Unfortunately the coming of the reaping machine and the binder left nothing to glean.

WHEN THE FAMILY FELL ON HARD TIMES

There was not even the minimum certain security for a family in difficulties. The welfare provided as of right to those in need was not to be developed until after the Second World War and it was only with the interwar government under Lloyd George's premiership that the old age pension began. And so even in the happiest cottage home, thoughts of unemployment, sickness and old age still held terrors for the working man and his wife.

During this period, the position of people unable to keep themselves was without hope. Women and children were needed for seasonal work and it was heavily relied upon as an essential part of the family income. Anyone unable to support him or herself had to go into the Union. The horror of being taken into the workhouse in old age still echoed in the memories of the elderly into the 1960's and probably longer. Once inside elderly couples were separated to the male and female wards. They were rarely ever to see each other again. There were only few allowances for outdoor relief, stringently adhered to.

Heckington was fortunate in having local benefactors, who left money to help the poor and needy including the Rebecca Packe charity which funded the Poor Row cottages opposite Burton Lane end (pulled down in the late 1960's) which must have been a godsend for the homeless. Also the almshouses the Godson family provided on the green and on Cameron Street.

The team of workmen photographed during the construction of the Godson almshouses on the Village Green.

There was also the provision of allotments; a new initiative in the 19th century. The idea arose following a national movement, as a way of providing families left landless with a basis for growing their own food and supplementing their limited incomes. It was suggested that 1 Rood (approx. 1/4 an acre) should be allotted to each tenant at an annual rent of 10s. a Rood. However, upon representation it was decided that 2 Roods might be more appropriate. A plough was usually hired for its cultivation.

The people of Heckington like many other rural communities also banded together to form clubs to insure themselves against loss of their pigs so vital to their household economy. The pig clubs and the sick and dividing clubs went some way to provide a little relief when illness hit the wage earner.

The dreaded green Dole Card.

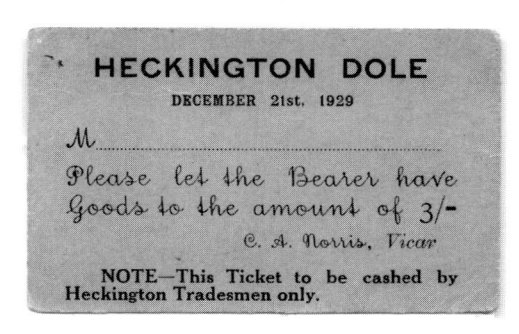

HECKINGTON DOLE
DECEMBER 21st, 1929
M............
Please let the Bearer have Goods to the amount of 3/-
C. A. Norris, Vicar
NOTE—This Ticket to be cashed by Heckington Tradesmen only.

VILLAGE LIVELIHOODS

With the increasing mass production of everyday needs in the factories of Victorian England cheap domestic goods in greater variety and easier access meant the gradual loss of the rural craftsman and one by one the craftsmen disappeared: the harness maker, the wheelwright, the tailor, the miller and the tinsmith. So it happened in Heckington, where we are rare in retaining our village blacksmith, a baker and a carpenter. But only these remain from a whole range of craftsmen that made Heckington a self-sufficient community little over a hundred years ago.

> 'The Lupton Family Last of the Tinkers Tinners and braziers to the people of Heckington 1859-1964'
> Generation after generation, both men and their widows carried on the craft of tinker through the good and the bad times.
> Margaret Bush, their descendant continues the story. "I can remember going with my Dad to measure people's 'blacklead grates' for new blowers or their ovens for dripping tins. There were no ready-made ones in those days. He used to do gas fitting as well. He used to make saucepans and steamers and the pans could be repaired three times with new bottoms. He also made tin kettles. Farmers used to bring cattle tanks to be mended and little boys their steam engines, which always had to be tried out before they were collected. He made drill tins for the blacksmith. These were a series of funnels joined together by chains through which the corn was sown. Another thing he enjoyed making were the water cans bound with brass bands, which the fairground folk used to have on their caravan steps. These weren't always profitable, as sometimes he was not paid until the following Feast.
> After my father's death in 1942, apart from a few soldering repairs I did for people, the workshop was not used again and the machinery sold, but my mother continued as an ironmonger until 1964, and then a family concern spanning at least 105 years finally came to an end." [Donaldson's Shop is where the Lupton's had their business]

There were also new forms of employment created by the new inventions. The Railway Company employed 18 men at the station, as porters, signalmen and platelayers. The coming of the railway acted as a catalyst for change and development in work patterns in other areas of the village economy allowing them to develop as they gained access to a much larger market. An obvious example of this growth is the way Charles Sharpe saw the potential opened up by the coming of the railway for rapid carriage of bulk freight to customers nationwide. He acted upon this rapidly in building the Pearoom where women were employed to sort peas for seed, which were loaded straight on to trucks coming right up to the Pearoom doors on a special siding.

LEISURE AND RECREATION
For the majority of families there was very little time for leisure and at the end of a day of heavy manual labour they had little energy for leisure activities. The Pubs were the meeting places for the men, where they could go for a pint with their mates. To the younger generation it might seem unbelievable but even until the middle of the 20th century women rarely went into a pub and then never unaccompanied by a man. In Victorian times it was unheard of for a woman to enter a pub. Heckington had no less than 10 pubs, including the two at East Heckington, which are recorded in this children's rhyme: -

HECKINGTON'S PUBS
Axe and Cleaver chop the sticks
Milk the Red Cow
Ride the White Horse
Ring the Six Bells
Wear the Crown
Bridle the Nag's Head
Climb the Royal Oak tree
Call at the Railway Hotel
Cut the Oat Sheaf
Spin the Wheel

> Despite so many lost drinking establishments, Heckington can perhaps make at least two modern additions to the list.
> "Play the Squash.
> Join the Club."

As with most villages at the time pubs and butchers shops were often found next door to each other, for the convenience of farmers, who could have a quick pint when bringing their beasts to be slaughtered. (Notice Heckington pub names, which reveal just such an association.) Sometimes the pints multiplied but as long as the farmer could be piled in his cart, the horse would take him home. No fear of breathalisation, and home by autopilot.

The Temperance Movement: Drunkenness was a very serious social problem in the Victorian era. This was caused by cheap spirits coming into common use rather than beer. Heckington was fortunate in having Doctor Moses Frank

MRCS in the village who was not only concerned but actually did something about it. He led the Temperance Movement. It launched with a Tea Meeting held on 19th January 1849. The venue was Brice's Hotel. It started with 10 members who paid 6d per week. Subsequent meetings were held in the Wesleyan Reform Chapel until they were frowned upon by the Elders as 'irreligious'. In response Dr Franks built the temperance hall at his own expense as an alternative meeting place. He gave the hall to the village when he left.

The members of the Temperance Group photographed on the Village Green

Temperance Revival 1910
It all started in the Axe & Cleaver [junction of Howell Road and Cameron Street) There had just been a General Election and the landlady was taunting some men because the candidate they favoured had not been elected. They left the inn, called a meeting and pledged themselves not to drink anything intoxicating for a year.
The idea caught on, and in a few days most of the men in the village had signed the pledge. Not all of them kept it, but many of them did, and some of them kept it to the end of their lives. The papers were full of it and it made news and big headlines in all the national papers. An enlarged photograph was exhibited in a shop window in the High street, and I remember as a small girl pressing my nose to the window glass, and feeling so proud because my Dad's name was there. The Hall was open on Saturday nights and everyone was welcome, and I loved Saturday night.

The Temperance Hall was the place for temperance teas and later for showing films - 'Saturday night at the Flicks' a real treat. The hall was also the scene of some highly cultural events arranged by William Little. I wonder what the villagers made of it all?

> William Little's own account of some events which he organised in the Hall
> Mr & Mrs Patey (very famous singer) arrived to spend a few days; a great musical treat on 19th September when Mr & Mrs Patey sang at a concert in the Peoples Hall and Walter Graham came from London to take part. It was a great treat and such as no other village in England could boast of [I really do not think this is any exaggeration!!!]
> 23rd January 1866 I gave a lecture at The People's Hall on the Sun and other scientific subjects. 20th January 1868 I delivered at the Peoples Hall a lecture on 'The Wonders of the Heavens' to a very crowded audience, but I fear the subject although assisted with the Magic Lantern would be complex and tedious to many. [not quite a Power Point Presentation but with computer games, television, the radio and cinema still to be invented it must have been quite a night out for the village]

The only other meeting places were those provided by the Church and the chapels. There were few holidays; those that there were, were looked forward to with happy anticipation and remembered with pleasure.

A wedding photograph taken outside the house of Jolly Stokes.

Most important were family occasions such as weddings, the chapel anniversaries and social events centred round the Church, for example this precursor of the show on its present site; 25th July 1865. A great day at Heckington. The Sleaford Volunteers held a review and dined in a tent in the Rookery. A bazaar in aid of church funds and a concert in the evening with remarkably fine weather and a great number of visitors make this a wonderful 30th July 1887 Heckington Feast, flower show, organ opening. The flower show held in the Rookery.

Fun and games for Children and Young People
No Disneyland experiences, no Jungle Gym, no adventure playgrounds or swimming baths, but the infinite adventure of exploring at will the fields and hedges and dykes of the village.

The ladies in the tea tent photographed in a much more genteel age.

The white elephant stall at an event held in the Hall gardens. *From left to right;* Miss C.Godson, Miss M.Godson, Mrs Newcombe, Miss M. Tomlinson and the Reverend Charles Arthur Norris.

How many ponds are left now? How easy is it to fish for minnows and tiddlers? How many hedgerows with a rich diversity of habitats? To quote one childhood memory. 'At Eastertide we used to go down to Boughton woods and pick violets. We would come back with huge bunches of both blue and white violets for our mothers'

Of course there were the Sunday school treats and feast celebrations. What fun was had and informal games with hoops and skipping rope down the Elm Holt.

Music always seems to have played a part in village life and there are reports of a choral society of very high standard. The Temperance band, later to be known as the Heckington town band was in the County tradition of brass band playing. 'A first class band under a first class Bandmaster Harry Money.'

The children in their 'Sunday best' preparing for a chapel event.

The fair has come to the Green and everyone looks forward to a rare day of recreation.

In the Elm Holt the throngs of local children create their own recreation.

Sports were varied. There were village cricket matches and in those colder winters skating on the frozen land, a skill and tradition echoing back to pre-fen drainage days and a sport for every one. William Little records on the 3rd January 1867: "Weather very severe, skating everywhere."

The Heckington Temperance Movement Band photographed in the grounds of D.G.Harris's house Saint Andrew's Villa in the late 1800s.

William Little gives us an insight into some other sporting events enjoyed by many of the gentlemen farmers of the village:

November Coursing at Ben Smiths - fine coursing - fine weather - and plenty of hares. December: Coursing at George's. Good sport

May 23rd Mr P. Graham here for the rook shooting (I imagine there may have been some very tasty rook pies after the shoot)

April 1866 Rook's nests 330 - 1865 275 nests - 275 nests - 1864 230 nests - 1863 only 180 nests. The rookery to the south side of the Hall grounds of course still exists. I wonder how many nests there are today?

The Cultural Life of the village centred around William Little and his family.

He records in May 1866 Mrs Lance here to visit us; the widow of Mr G Lance the eminent fruit painter.

September 1866 Allen Duncan son of the celebrated artist is here. He has made several good sketches and in the same month, " Mr N Lockyer a Fellow of the Astronomical Society has come for a few days."

March 1887 Went to London for the sale of my large picture "The Crimean Heroes" at Christie & Mansons.

A house party at the Hall in 1874.
Standing. W.Little.
Seated rear; C.Guys, E.Little, M.A.Little, W.Little jr, M.Ingram.
Front; A.G.Meredith, E.Garrod, M.G.Jordan and W.Phillips.

A selection of Roman field walking finds including roof tile, pottery and the inevitable oyster shell.

Fragments of the rough clay vessels used in Roman Heckington for boiling sea water to extract the salt.

Low dark mounds of salt making debris next to the A17 near Garwick. These salterns once lay next to salt water creeks.

A magnificent spearhead, no doubt sadly missed by its Bronze Age owner. Found by Mark Sardeson close to Heckington Beck.

A delicate flint blade found by field walkers in Star Fen.

A battered stone axehead found by field walkers near Side Bar Lane. This type of axe was being made in far off Langdale some 4,000 years ago.

A narrow blade and a round scraper made from black flint found in Star Fen.

The Langdale Pikes in the Lake District. The axe factory was situated on the light coloured band of scree to the upper left of the peak.

The seal from a glass bottle showing an unidentified coat of arms. Found near the site of Cobham Hall.

71

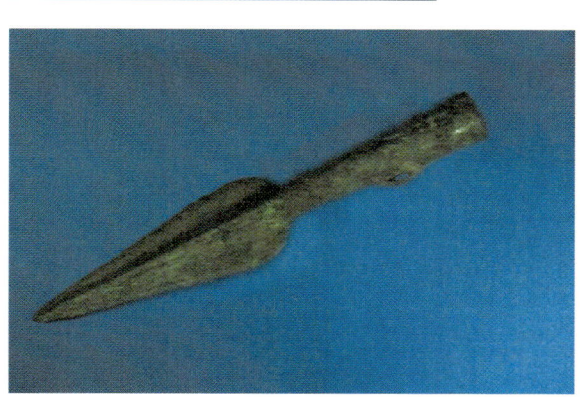

Above is a copy of the portraits of the medieval lord of the manor Sir Henry de Beaumont and his wife, formerly Lady Grantham. The original copy was done in 1641 just before the destructive times of the civil war.

To the left is a photograph of the medieval wall painting which still survives in Saint Andrew's Church Asgarby. It is described as a kneeling robed figure with scrolled text on a deep red ground spangled with white flowers.

The leadwork plaque still in the Church depicting the names of Henry Farrar and William Taylor who were Churchwardens in 1681.

Cawdron family brasses taken from old tombstones in the floor of the Church and mounted on a pillar to preserve them. To John Cawdron, died 1488 and William Cawdron, died 1544. 'Sumtyme Baylyf of Hekyngton'

Photograph of a moulded stone from an earlier building of Winkhill Hall and dated 1638.

73

Above is a copy of a watercolour of the 'inkpot' by Karl Wood. This house used to stand approximately where the entrance to Potesgrave Way is now and was nicknamed as such because of its unusual shape. It is reproduced here by permission of the Usher Gallery Lincoln. Below is Toby Cottage down Church Street which is a good example of ancient mud and stud construction. It had a thatched roof until a few years ago.

The art of mud and stud construction is not lost, as demonstrated here at the 2001 Heckington Show.

Above is a copy of a watercolour by Karl Wood and reproduced by permission of the Usher Gallery, Lincoln. It depicts Winkhill Manor House. It was rebuilt in brick in 1780 with the ancient coat of arms taken from the previous building and resited on the front of the new one.

To the right is a copy of a watercolour and pencil painting of a Lincolnshire Draining Mill by John Sell Cotman 1782-1842. It was a gift to the Cecil Higgins Art Gallery, Bedford, England, with whose permission it is reproduced here.

The Manor and the Church viewed from the northeast where Godson Avenue now stands. Although painted in 1853 it shows a scene that had changed little since the 17th and 18th centuries.

Some notable details are: The men harvesting corn with sickles. The long straw for thacking corn stacks and graving potatoes also winter bedding for cattle. The Church with the flat roof which was fitted in the 1400s and wasn't to be replaced until 1866. The Manor House rebuilt in around 1700. The hedges and large elm trees. The horse and carriage in front of the Manor house. The thatched roofs of the house and barn in front of the Church.

The original watercolour is the work of Samuel Read, one of the leading artists for the Illustrated London News. No doubt he came to visit Heckington with his employer William Little who was co- founder of the newspaper and whose wife Elizabeth Godson was born in the Manor House.

WWII items. Home Guard armband, Lincs Reg't cap Badge, Flying helmet, Anti Aircraft shell, Lee Enfield Bayonet, Mills grenade, Jack knife, Rifle ammo & 20mm cannon shells. Photo by Pat Banister 2001.

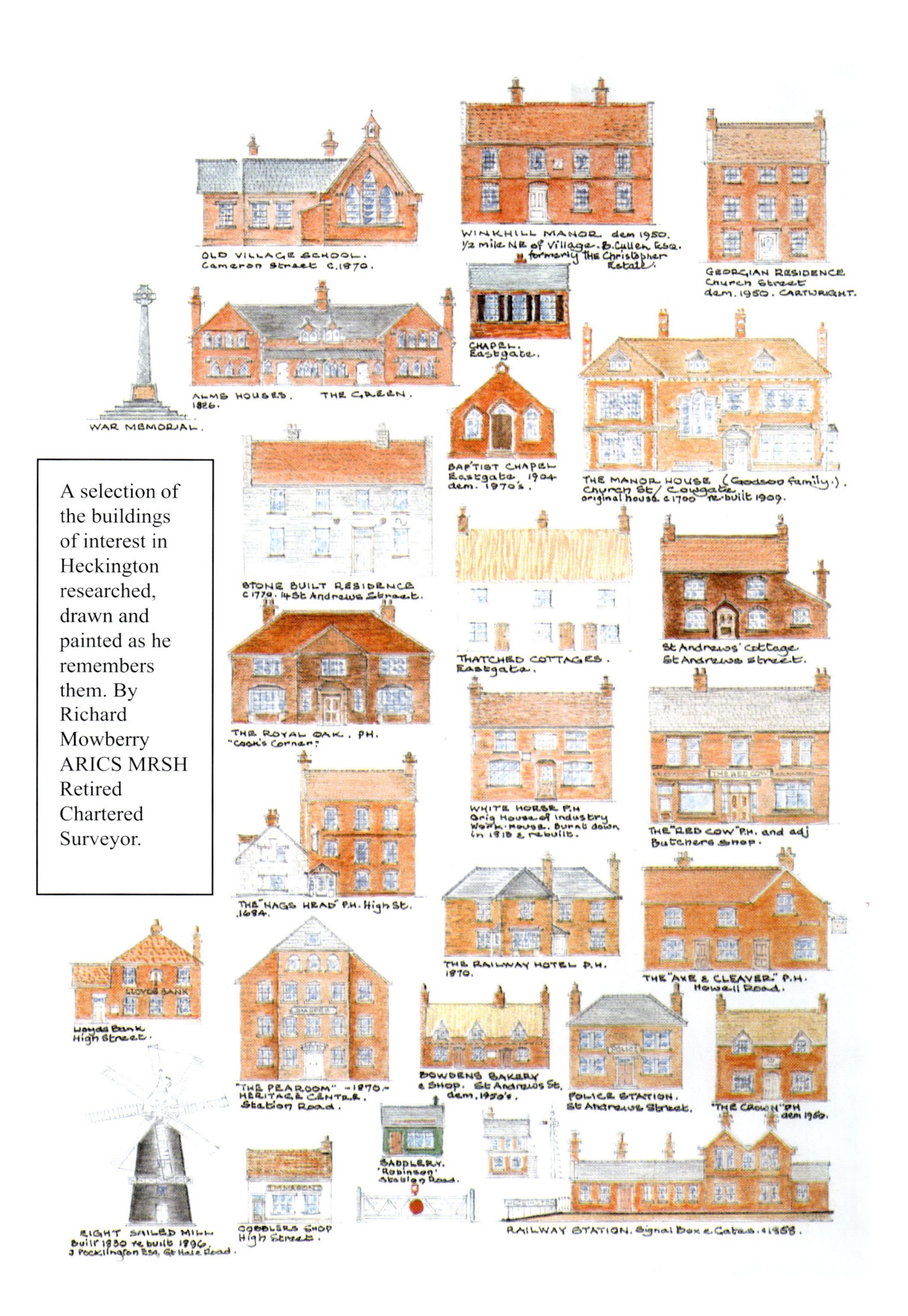

A selection of the buildings of interest in Heckington researched, drawn and painted as he remembers them. By Richard Mowberry ARICS MRSH Retired Chartered Surveyor.

OLD VILLAGE SCHOOL. Cameron Street c.1870.

WINKHILL MANOR. dem 1950. ½ mile NE of Village. B.Cullen Esq. formerly THE Christopher Estate.

GEORGIAN RESIDENCE Church Street dem. 1950. CARTWRIGHT.

ALMS HOUSES. THE GREEN. 1826.

CHAPEL. Eastgate.

WAR MEMORIAL.

BAPTIST CHAPEL Eastgate. 1904 dem. 1970's.

THE MANOR HOUSE (Godson family.) Church St / Cowgate. original house c1700 re-built 1909.

STONE BUILT RESIDENCE c.1770. 14 St Andrews Street.

THATCHED COTTAGES. Eastgate.

St Andrews' Cottage St Andrews Street.

THE ROYAL OAK. P.H. "Cook's Corner."

WHITE HORSE P.H. Orig House of Industry Work. House. Burnt down in 1918 & rebuilt.

THE "RED COW" P.H. and adj Butchers Shop.

THE "NAGS HEAD" P.H. High St. 1684.

THE RAILWAY HOTEL P.H. 1870.

THE "AXE & CLEAVER." P.H. Howell Road.

Lloyds Bank High Street.

"THE PEAROOM" – 1870 – HERITAGE CENTRE. Station Road.

BOWDENS BAKERY & SHOP. St Andrews St. dem. 1950's

POLICE STATION. St Andrews Street.

"THE CROWN" P.H. dem 1960.

EIGHT SAILED MILL. Built 1830 re-built 1896. J. Pocklington Esq. Gt Hale Road.

COBBLERS SHOP High Street.

SADDLERY. 'Robinson' Station Road.

RAILWAY STATION. Signal Box & Gates. c.1858.

77

The Pinfold as it is today with the flower and herb garden.

Looking out across Butts Hill from Station Road before the housing development.

RELIGION

During this period and particularly in the early part there was much activity centred round the restoration of the fabric of the church, which had been allowed to fall into considerable dereliction in the preceding 100 years. This situation reflects that in much of the country.

On 9th November 1865 a meeting for the restoration of the Church was held at which the vicar Rev Cameron increased his already substantial personal subscription to £500. The project moved on quickly, by April of the following year meetings were being held to inspect plans and estimates for the restoration. The restoration fund had by that time grown to £2,200, enough to put a new roof on the church other than the side aisles, the transepts and chancel, only an additional £300 being needed to repair all the windows and so advertisements were placed for tenders.

This photograph of the Church taken before the programme of renovation and restoration was given to Michael Cole Sumners by William Little.

By May a meeting was held to open the tenders. The work listed to be done was general repairs of outside of church - reroofing nave, reglazing all the windows repairing and restoring windows - scraping inside [this is when the last of the plaster and wall paintings were lost] - and if required the North and South aisles. This left only the reroofing of the chancel and North and South aisles to complete the church. This had to wait until 1886 when it was financed by a bequest in Henry Godson's will.

The contract was given to Donington's the builders and the church was closed on 10th June. On the 11th the pews, pulpit etc. were removed and work began within a fortnight. The reopening of the restored Church took place on 30th April 1867. William Little comments 'most unfortunate weather, appearance of a cold rainy and miserable day. Surely such weather on such occasions should teach us that natures laws are immutable.' then adds - 'the afternoon has turned out very fine'.

This copy of a lithograph of Saint Andrew's Church shows it just after the restoration of the pitched roof.

The other major church building projects of the time were the construction of a church at East Heckington and the building of a new Methodist Church in Church Street in 1905.

The opening of the new Methodist Church was quite an occasion as the photograph illustrates.

The new Church at East Heckington. The war memorial which now stands to the left of the entrance has yet to be built.

EDUCATION

In earlier centuries only the very wealthy and scribes in the churches could read and write. Private tutors taught the children of the wealthy at home. Then in Tudor England grammar schools were founded by wealthy merchants to ensure that there were some literate and numerate boys who would be available to ensure the proper conduct of the world of power and commerce. Literally they were taught to read and write, study Latin and Greek, and do mathematics. Thus, Carre in Sleaford founded the grammar school. There were some scholarships to such schools and the better off would pay to send their sons. An advert of the 1840's announces that there are 'two masters both of whom are in Holy Orders. The course of education pursued at the school being similar to public schools in that each pupil has a separate bed'! The sons of the really wealthy would be sent to the developing Public Schools.

When first I came to Heckington in the early 1960's I was astounded to learn that until recently all village children other than those few passing their scholarship [11+] stayed at Heckington school until they left at 14 to start work. I remember the baker telling me that as he left school for the last time his father was waiting at the gate for him with a basket full of bread for delivery and he was a working man.

The first printed record we have of education in Heckington is in PIGOTS Directory of 1835 advertising the John Freiston Academy in Heckington and citing John Freiston as an expert in calligraphy.

By 1842 Rev Lefevre is running a 'Sunday school in Heckington -literally a school on Sunday being the one day when working people had any free time. The Baptists started schools on Sundays and prided themselves on the quality of education, which they provided.

In 1846 The National School was founded and from then on gradually became the main school in the village housed in the buildings on the corner of Cameron Street (now the Heritage Lincs). It was built at a cost of £450 and provided 112 places. Income of the National School was its Government Grant+ scholars fees of 2d per week supplement, occasionally by a 'sermon collection' 1849. For those with means Carres Grammar School was a possibility. There was a voluntary subscription scheme for places, but the vicar Charles de la Cour reported in 1851 that fewer than half the places had been taken up as the scheme was every unpopular and *"resulted in parents sending their children to other schools in preference.*

Looking down what was then Chapman Street with the school and schoolhouse on the right.

The 1851 census records only one hundred of the 402 village children between four and 14 years of age were listed as "scholars". Of these, governesses taught some at home. Some attended Mr Barker's private day school on the village green, while others were day scholars at the two private boarding schools on the High Street. Ten farm labourer's children were receiving some sort of education, probably at the National School. The National school had a School Master and Mistress only with no assistants or Monitors. Teacher training was only just beginning. The annual salary of the schoolmaster was £320 per annum and that of his wife the Schoolmistress £18.15s. They occupied the schoolhouse and garden rent-free and coal, insurance and rates cost them £8.33s annually. In 1851 [Census return] Charles de la Cour commenting on The Return of Schools and Scholars suggests the school should be put on a more permanent basis. A Master and Mistress of a higher class should be employed and the character of a poor Parish school should be done away with. Charles de la Cour provided from his own pocket funding for a Sunday school (literally a school on Sunday). Until very recently there was a box in Church house marked Sunday School and which had survived from this period.

A very early school photograph taken by Ben Smith who had a shop and photographic business on the High Street.

At this time there was also a Wesleyan Sunday school and a private school in the village as well as two Dames Schools. Additionally there were two families who employed governesses the Godson's and that of Charles de la Cour. We know nothing of these particular governesses, but frequently they were middle-class women in reduced circumstances, whose own education was very limited.

From the 1870 census returns we have evidence of a boarding school being run by the Misses Dobson at Heckington Hall They had nine girl boarders aged 9-17. The Hall was opposite the Post Office where Jubilee Terrace now stands. Next door, at the Red House, which was a boarding school run by Miss Mary Hoole, sister of the village vet. Here there were six boarding scholars, including one boy, aged 7-17.
In addition there were also several dame schools, some of which may have been run by dissenters. One was run by a Mrs Foster next door to the White Horse in Church Street. She must have kept the school open until 1882 when the last of her pupils was admitted to the National School.

Following the 1870 Education Act, the village school was again enlarged in 1873, providing an extra 80 places. The Victorian concept of school buildings was very different from that of today. There was a government Rule Book for School Planning and Fitting up. Rule 6 stated, *"An infant school should always be on the ground floor, and, if exceeding 80 children in number, should have two galleries of unequal size and a small group of benches and desks for the occasional use of the elder infants."* Rule 14 states, *"The sills of the windows should be placed not less than four feet above the floor."* Apparently the scholars were not to be allowed to waste their time looking out of the window during lessons.

The attendance at the National School continued to fluctuate greatly. Even after Schooling became compulsory in 1876. The weather played a major part in school attendance with children staying away in rough or rainy weather. Work on the land also kept many away according to the season. On 13th April 1869 the master commented in his logbook on low attendance, *"potato planting being considered of paramount importance just now"*. Other good excuses for non-attendance were *"Edmonds menagerie being on the village green"* (2nd December 1872) and *"the expected arrival of more parties of the 7th Dragoons"* (28th April 1873).

Having said all that, we know that some families went to extraordinary extents to get their education. The Minkleys, who lived in Heckington Fen, had a family with seven children of school age in the 1930s. Rural poverty during the Depression was such that the four eldest were sent to school wearing boots, but then three of the children had to take off their boots when they got to the village school. This was so that the eldest child could walk back to the house and deliver the boots to the three remaining children so they in turn could get to school. The whole procedure was played out in reverse at the end of each school day.

Heckington School 1893 - 1903

I started in the infants' section of the school in 1893 at the age of 3 and left in 1903. So I had 10 years continuous schooling under the headmastership of John Nichols and I have always regarded his reign as a vintage period because he and his wife did try and I think succeeded in turning out from pretty raw material, something which can truthfully be described as successful people. Some of us became pharmaceutical chemists, no mean achievement in those days. One started a very successful business for farmers and businessmen in the United States of America. Another became an important man in a retail business in Regina Canada.

In fact in the period of some fifteen years the groundwork was provided on which a good number of boys and girls built successful careers. It was Mr Nichols who when I was 15 years old insisted that I took on the job of being the local correspondent for the Sleaford Mercury. When I left school just after my 13th birthday I could recite Portia's speech from the Merchant of Venice, the poem beginning 'You are old Father William' from Alice, had acquaintance with algebra, tonic solfa, and we were all good at mental arithmetic and understood those damned dots of the decimal system.

In the winter months we had 'evening classes' really a form of continuous education. Also Mr & Mrs Nichols conducted dancing classes in the winter on Friday evenings for we young people with a long evening once a month and a 'ball' at the end of the season. Music was provided by Elizabeth and Harry Money whose father carried on the business of wheelwright in the premises next door to the old school house. It must be remembered that when we left the village school that was the end of formal education for almost all of us.

The class of 24th July 1917.

Headmaster Mr (Teddy) Corlett who 'ruled' for many years in the early 1900s. His staff in 1917 *from left to right;* Miss F.Hessell from Great Hale, Mrs Reed, Miss Giblett from New Street, Miss E.Pidd and Miss G.Money.

SCHOOL CONCERT 1908

"Mr Corlett, the Headmaster trained us. We had a new platform made by the Money family, with two tiers of seats like the show stands, with a gangway in the middle. I am sure there would be well over a hundred boys and girls taking part. The Dowager Countess of Winchilsea, who lived in the Dower House at Ewerby, came with her guests. Mrs Allinson, the vicar's wife brought visitors and of course all the Godsons, Littles and Tomlinsons. They paid us the compliment of coming in evening dress and jewels; the Countess sported a tiara. As you will imagine I was greatly impressed by all this splendour. I wore my summer cream dress, made out of one of Auntie May's old ones, three rows of corals, white shoes and stockings. The song I sang in was, "Gossip Joan". At the end of our song, we danced a short Minuet and did a curtsey, which Mrs Allinson taught us after school closed. My brother and I think two more boys sat on stools and sang "I'm forever blowing bubbles", they had basins of soapsuds and clay pipes. There was a Negro song, "Poor Old Joe" and Jessie Barnatt was Dinah, dressed in a black dress, white apron with plain bib. The star turn was a crippled girl called Olive Maidens, who really could hit the top notes. As she was on crutches I was told to look after her from her arriving to going home. Her brothers used to bring her to school in a mail cart, very funny pram, seat back and front with long handles. Cecil Dickinson's little girls all wore nighties and carried candles in blue candlesticks. At the interval we had huge plates of oranges handed round cut in quarters. We had one quarter each. These had all been cut up and prepared by the three teachers, who were our dressers and backroom girls. Miss Coulson Deputy Head, Miss Bradley and Miss Nellie Holmes. The plates were passed around again to collect the peel etc. I also remember Mr Corlett on the concert nights did not give us any vocal instructions, all were given by striking cords on the piano. He certainly had us well trained, but what a lot of hard work he must have put in for weeks and the teachers as well. Unfortunately some of the boys of that generation were killed in the First World War, Jessie Barnatt for instance.

Even in those very early days school wasn't all work and no play. Ada Priestly is the fifth girl from the left.

TRANSPORT

Until the middle of the 19th century the only means of transport was by foot or by horse. Since then transport and mobility have improved tremendously, but not without cost. The first big change was the opening of the railway through Heckington on 12th April 1859. The line was built by the Boston, Sleaford & Midland Counties Railway, running from Boston to Grantham. Its primary purpose was to link the port of Boston with the factories and coalmines of the East Midlands, but it was also to bring considerable change to the village. For many, travel became affordable for the first time, for both short and long journeys.

A very early photograph of Heckington railway station.

Demand for travel to Sleaford on market day was so great, that on 16th May 1859, 100 people were left behind on Heckington Station. The railway company refused to return their fares and there followed *"a scene of disorder and dissatisfaction"*. In 1873, a party of school children from nearby Asgarby and Kirkby Laythorpe visited Skegness *"most of them having never been to the seaside or so far from home before"*. The railway brought progress in other ways.

Coal could now be brought in cheaply, enabling a gasworks to be established, owned and managed by village residents. Curiously, it was sited some distance from the station, at the junction of Vicarage Road and Cowgate. Coal had to be transported through the village by horse and cart, contracted out to the Taylor family, the landlords of the Axe and Cleaver. Coal for domestic use was more readily available, and ultimately, four coal merchants established depots at the station.

The pattern of road traffic changed. After 1860, tolls charged to travellers were insufficient to cover running costs, and in 1876, the turnpike trust was dissolved. The maintenance of these roads reverted to the parish. The level of local traffic increased as more goods were taken to or from the railway station. Personal mobility was improved by the bicycle, both for business and pleasure. By 1894, Heckington had a Bicycle Club, where members enjoyed an evening outing to Billingborough, some 10 miles away. Activity was sufficient to support a bicycle shop in the village. Local travel was also provided by the two village carriers, Joseph Bancroft and Samuel Holmes, who took their horse drawn vehicles to Sleaford and Boston, carrying people and parcels, and running errands.

The age of private personal transport was here and Almond's cycle shop was to fulfil the need. Right in the centre of the village the shop was where Harvest Insurance is now.

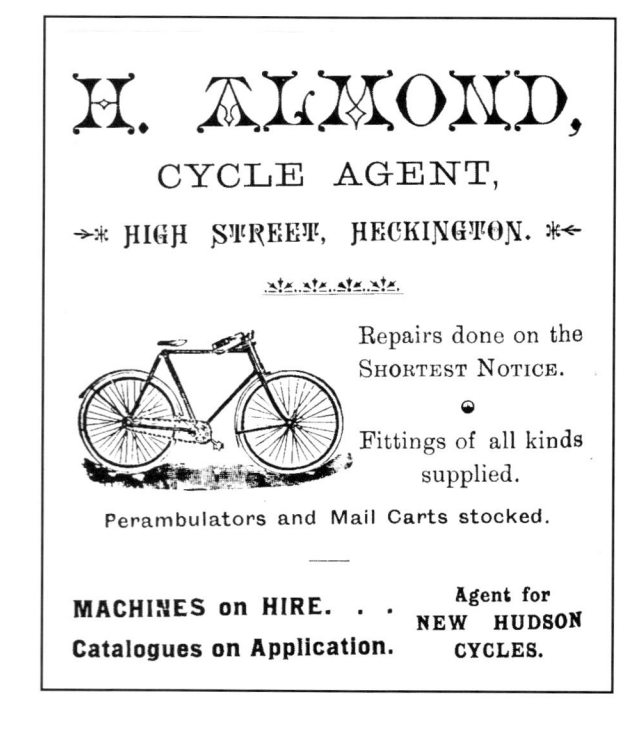

H. ALMOND,

CYCLE AGENT,

HIGH STREET, HECKINGTON.

Repairs done on the SHORTEST NOTICE.

Fittings of all kinds supplied.

Perambulators and Mail Carts stocked.

MACHINES on HIRE. . .

Catalogues on Application.

Agent for NEW HUDSON CYCLES.

> As late as 8th September 1896 there was a report in the local paper that two traveling minstrels visited Heckington. They were performing in a village inn and came into conversation with a local pig dealer. The minstrels had a child with them and during the conversation offered the child for sale to the man. A deal was struck and after the minstrels had inspected the pig dealers home to ensure that it was suitable to bring the child up in they sold the child to the pig dealer for one shilling!

At the turn of the century, the first motor vehicles appeared - the first one in the village being owned by Ernest Henry Godson, who lived at the Manor in Church Street. Harold Cook remembered this particular car breaking down just by their blacksmith's shop at Cook's corner. It had a blown gasket but Harold's father made a temporary gasket of thick brown paper saturated with thick machine oil, which apparently worked extremely well. By the 1920's, the Almonds had expanded their cycle shop to include a coach service, which was carried on by their successors, Sharpe's Motors until the 1980's.

The Lincolnshire Road Car Company also ran a service from Sleaford until the mid-1970's. As car ownership increased, long distance traffic through the village increased, spawning several petrol stations to meet its needs. The level of traffic began to cause concern, and as early as 1938 a bypass for the village was proposed. The Second World War caused this to be abandoned. It was not until 1982 that the bypass was finally opened, after some strenuous campaigning by village residents. They even conducted their own traffic survey. Since that time traffic within the village has grown again as the population and level of car ownership has risen. People also miss out on contact with other people they would meet when walking around the village, as in the old days.

Now with fewer family and work ties within the village and fewer people walking around to shop and visit we are going to have to work consciously at getting to know one another and keeping the fantastic sense of community which has held our community together so positively for thousands of years and has remained the same what ever else has changed.

CHAPTER SIX

THE SECOND WORLD WAR

1939 and the advent of what was to become known as World War II brought a good deal of change to Heckington as it did to most places. As in the Great War many of the young men of the village volunteered or were called up into the armed forces, and as before there were those who did not return, or who returned with visible or mental scars.

However, being a rural farming community there were those who served their country in other ways. By staying behind to work on the farms and in the munitions factories at places like the British Manufacturing and Armaments Company (MARCOs) at Grantham. Their military experience comprised service in the Local Defence Volunteers, known rather light heartedly as *Look Duck and Vanish.* Formed in May 1940 the local founder member and Commanding Officer was Mr. J.E. Taylor who was also the Headmaster of Heckington school. The LDV was renamed The Home Guard in July of the same year and Mr. Taylor was awarded a commission as a Major. Mr. Smalley the local insurance agent was also commissioned though he later served in the forces. Some of the original Sergeants were Mr.Wesson the baker, Mr. Mowberry the undertaker and Mr. Beck Snr. Mr. Mowberry had to leave later as he had funeral contracts with the RAF. All those who were eligible and able from Heckington and all the outlying villages were to become members of the HG at some time. A number of them were eventually called to service, some never to return.

Mr J.E.Taylor, well respected headmaster of the village school and Major in the Home Guard during the Second world War.

Parade was held in the Railway Station yard every Sunday much to the delight of the local schoolchildren who would go along to watch drill practice.

Heckington also had its own fire service during the war with the engine at one time being kept in the Church but during the war the Fire Station was at the rear of Church House which was then known as the Reading Room. It was equipped with a small and antiquated fire engine and a number of stirrup pumps. All under the auspices of Jack Scoggins. Many of them worked at Scoggins woodyard on the Sleaford Road, which made it handy if there was a callout.

The village policeman at the time was Constable Tear who had been called back from 'war reserve' having previously retired. He served for the duration of hostilities assisted by Special Constables Ben Levesly, Monty Read, Mark Lawson, George Sharman and Bill Porter, though there were others.

Heckington at this time must have been teeming with people in uniforms of one sort or another as there was also the Royal Observer Corps. They were known as Easy Three No 11 Group ROC. The lookout post was at Great Hale and down a farm road off to the right as you go into the village. Amongst others this was staffed by Charlie Beck, Richard Mowberry, Bob Colby and those pictured below.

Members of the ROC pose for a group photograph near their post at Great Hale, with the Church and the mill in the background. *Back row from left to right;* G.Jeffery, G.W.Pope, F.V.Housley, W.N.Anderson, G.W.Dunmore, H.Mowberry, A.Gilbert. *Middle;* D.J.Collins, J.P.Hubbard, J.Scoggins, C.Bell. *Front row;* G.Dobbs, S.Dawson.

Of course we mustn't forget the Air Raid Precautions team who it is reported would 'make a hell of a noise if they saw a chink of light.' Notable names staffing this department were Mr.Stephenson Snr, Mr.Mason and Mr.Coaton.

Their job was to ensure a complete blackout in the village at night for fear of detection by enemy bombers.

The Army came to the village within days of the war breaking out and consisted of a Battery of The Royal Artillery. They brought with them Quads, Limbers and rather antiquated field Guns. Quads were a peculiar type of enclosed lorry, which were designed to tow the Limbers and Guns. The Limbers were an ammunition carrier, which fitted between the Quad and the Gun.

The soldiers were billeted all over the village in lofts, barns and outhouses. The battery office was the yellow brick house opposite the Church near the entrance to Newton's Yard. The Navy Army & Airforce Institute (The NAAFI was the recreational catering organisation.) was the Reading Room in Saint Andrew's Street. The Guardroom was in Cameron Street. The Village Hall was the Other Ranks Mess and the Red Cow was the Sergeants' Mess. Heckington House on the Boston Road was the Officers' Mess whilst the Guns and Vehicles were kept under armed guard down Eastgate. This was later to evolve into a section of the 1st Airlanding Battery. Sadly many were lost during the Arnhem landings but of the survivors there were those who not only fell in love with Heckington and the surrounding area but also with the lovely local lasses. These too were destined to settle here. For many years Arnhem reunions were held with old comrades returning to reminisce, remember and visit old friends. But time marches on and sadly but inevitably those returning got fewer and fewer until the last official church service and parade was held in the summer of 1999. Despite this there are still a few who come back every year.

The final official Church parade of the Arnhem Veterans photographed in 1999 by Pat Banister.

What with all this, and the skies being full of wave after wave of Lancaster Bombers going out and often limping home, then American Bombers doing the same thing, Heckington must have been a vastly different place from what it is today.

Next to come was the Air Training Corps. This was originally formed by Mr. Pearson who was an Air Ministry Civil Servant at RAF Cranwell. He was awarded a Commission as a Pilot Officer. Their HQ was at one time in the second cottage from the corner in the houses that stood on the corner of Cameron Street and Vicarage Road near the old school. The section was later taken over by Mr. Cropp who was another Civil Servant. He is remembered as being 'a man with an uncanny knack of handling young men in the best way possible, a leader as opposed to a driver.' 'It was at this time that the ATC really got the cream of the village into their ranks.'

Eventually there was to be a custom built HQ down the lane that is now Lime Tree Walk which continued in operation into the late fifties when Squadron Leader Cropp retired. Not long after in 1960, again with Squadron Leader Cropp's assistance, it emerged as number 2160 Sleaford Squadron ATC and is still going strong at its HQ down the Drove in Sleaford.

As the war in Europe dragged on and more and more things were put on ration everyone with even the smallest piece of ground turned it into garden for the production of food. This was when the keeping of the family pig at the bottom of the garden became a distinct advantage and every spare morsel of waste went into the swill bucket. One of the small mercies of life in a rural community was that by a series of 'horse trades' and barter most families got at least some of the items they needed.

> A pig was treated like one of the family until it was large enough for slaughter. There was no room for sentiment then.

In 1942 busloads of schoolchildren were being brought in to the village from as far away as London to help with the potato picking. Split into groups they were sent to the various farms and slept on straw mattresses in the barns. Daphne Pearson, now living near Nottingham remembers this well.

93

As time went on and more enemy prisoners were captured, several internment camps were built in the area. This brought some relief from the labour shortage when the German and Italian prisoners began to be shipped out to the local farms by lorry each morning to help with the harvest of corn, sugar beet and potatoes. This in itself brought more change to the village as by the end of the hostilities romances had flourished and there were weddings between local girls and some of the prisoners. Many couples settled down and raised families in the village, some spending all their lives here, working hard for the community and serving as parish councillors.

A group of German prisoners. Third from the left is Willelm Gustaf Hunsdorfer. He stayed on in the village, married a local girl and went on to become a parish councillor.

Some young girls from the community joined the Women's Land Army and were posted as far afield as Devon and Cornwall, while land girls from the north midlands were in turn posted here. Again romances flourished and the end of the war saw local lads from the farms marrying girls with northern accents.

Even long after the end of the war its effects could still be seen on the farms and in the fields, where the severe shortage of proper agricultural machinery meant that some of the farmers were using stripped down tanks, armoured personnel carriers and half-track vehicles to pull their ploughs and seed drills. For a good many years the farm workers could be seen dressed in a mixture of army surplus and civvies and carrying khaki webbing lunch bags slung over their shoulders as they cycled to work.

It was at this time that the Boy Scouts had their HQ in a Nissen hut at the bottom of Foster Street where the bungalows are now. There are generations of Heckington lads who have fond memories of Mr. (Skip) Crosby the Scoutmaster who ran it with great dedication for many years.

The 1st Heckington Boy Scout Troop photographed in the early 1950s. In the background is the Nissen hut HQ and the rear of one of Sharpe's Luxury Coaches. On the left is Scoutmaster Richard Crosby Snr, at the rear is Reverend Skelton and to the right assistant Scoutmaster Pat Line. They are about to set off for summer camp. The photograph is dated at around 1955.

However time and civilization marches on. The world is as they say 'a different place.' Heckington though scarred and changed survived the war and has grown almost beyond recognition. As this is being written, after 56 years, war is once more rearing its ugly head. Let us sincerely hope that our village is not as badly scarred again.

No book on Heckington would be complete without mention of the village show, so over the page follows a short history starting from its very beginnings and bringing us up to the present day.

Probably the oldest and longest running village show in the country. It's highly probable that the show's history can be traced back almost a thousand years. These shows as we know them invariably evolved during Victorian times from the feast days, which were held on or around the patron Saint's Day of the Church.

It is believed that the Church of Saint Mary Magdalene was completed on the site in 1104. This is probably the reason that the show is celebrated at the end of July and not 20th November, which is Saint Andrew's day the patron saint of the present Church. The patronage was recorded as being changed to Saint Andrew in 1864. The full dedication title is to 'Saint Andrew, Saint Mary Magdalene and All Saints'.

For hundreds of years the feast days were just that. Together with Church attendance and religious observance cattle would be slaughtered, food prepared and recreational games played. Bowling for a pig is one of the skittles competitions that has travelled down the ages and is still occasionally practiced. At a time of very few holidays for the ordinary working person it was a great day to be looked forward to and prepared for. Probably the only other day off during the year would be Christmas day.

It was the Victorians who really developed the idea of an organised show. The first Flower Show being held on Feast Tuesday 28th July 1863 two months after the foundation of the Heckington Horticultural Society by Ernest Godson. It is reported that the event was held in a marquee erected on the bowling green and there were 28 classes of fruit, flowers and vegetables. Unfortunately it cannot be ascertained with any certainty where the Bowling Green was at that time. It has been suggested that it could have meant The Village Green however it's believed that the fair began here in the 1850s and there probably wouldn't have been room for both. Wherever the venue it was considered to have been a great success and plans were made for it to continue the next year.

In 1864 there were two marquees on the site and also a concert in the Temperance Hall. Horticultural classes were up to 50 and there were also craft exhibits. It was noted in the local press that there was considerably less rowdyism and drunkenness than in years gone by.

The show was going from strength to strength and over the next few years there were exhibitions of hothouse plants and paintings by the local gentry. The biggest step forward came in 1867 when William Little offered the Hall Grounds as a venue. There was now room to hold penny-farthing cycle racing which it did in 1869 as well as an evening dance on the Hall lawns. This was lit by gas jets in 1872 when the firework displays began and by 1878 was lit by electricity. Not many years later came the equestrian events and hurdling, the forerunner to show jumping, together with horses trotting in harness. Houses and streets were festooned with bunting and streamers and the Heckington Town Band played as it marched round the village.

By the middle of the 1880s and continuing right up to the 1950s, Great Northern Railways were laying on special trains to take people back to Sleaford and Billingborough in the evening.

From about 1890 to 1900 things slackened off a bit. Interest was lost in the flower show. Gate receipts began to fall and the committee had to have a serious re-think. Ernest Godson who had been secretary from the start was tactfully made president and a new secretary, Mr A.J.Ollerhead appointed. Things began to look up again until the rain of 1904. The committee pulled through but 1907 was a complete washout. Despite this and a serious shortage of funds there was a show in 1908. The 1909 show was an utter disaster with pouring rain and only 192 people attending in the afternoon. Undeterred the committee organized a promenade concert in the Hall grounds in August. Helped out by Ruskington Town Band and Mr R.D.C. Shaw with his performing horses the society finished up with twenty pounds in the bank to carry on the next year.

With their troubles behind them from 1910 the show prospered again. Bigger and better than ever with the reintroduction of the Horticultural and Flower section, now divided into three sections for Professionals, Amateurs and Cottagers.

The years 1915 to 1918 were of course dormant; as were the years from 1939 to 44 due to the terrible world conflicts but other that this it had become a huge success. Generally this was to continue until the mid 50s. By 1959 the show had been losing money for several years and a radical rethink was needed. A meeting was held at the Nag's Head on 8th November 1960 and it was decided to call it a day.

In deciding to abandon the show the committee had failed to take into account the loyalty, enthusiasm and determination of the young people of Heckington. A petition was organised and they were asked to reconsider. Many of the old committee resigned and there was a good deal of trouble and strife with finances, equipment and assets but there was a grim determination by the 'new blood' to succeed. The upshot was that in 1964 a horticultural show was held in the Village Hall at the weekend, one hundred years after the first concert had been held there in 1864. This was a great success and by 1965 the show was back in the Hall grounds having moved from Tuesday to a two day event on Saturday and Sunday. The organisers found that it only cost 10% more to hire the flower tent for the extra day. The committee doing a great deal of the construction and layout work themselves kept costs to a minimum. This tradition has carried on to the present day with many of them taking their annual holidays to help with the construction and dismantling which all told takes about a fortnight to complete. The hard work and dedication of all those concerned over the years have made Heckington Show the success it is today with attendances of up to 12,000.

The photograph above was taken on 17th May 1947 by No 82 Squadron RAF and is reproduced by permission of English Heritage National Monuments Records Ref CPE/UK/2073 FR:4085.

This photograph was taken in the early 1970s and given to the Heckington Village trust by Mr. Gordon Brotherton.

This aerial photograph was taken at 11.30am on Sunday 12th September 1999 by Pat Banister

With these three aerial photographs we are attempting to compare the enormous changes that have taken place in the village over the last fifty years or so.

Top left taken in 1947 shows the village with little change for hundreds of years except for the beginnings of the Foster Street development which for many years was known by the locals as *The Cart Track*. Also the recently built Handley Street *Prefabs*. The Playing field is still tree covered parkland and the New School is a dense orchard. The round white dot of the Gas Holder on Cowgate is clearly visible as are the kitchen gardens and orchards of the Hall.

Bottom left we are looking west towards Sleaford with the Churchill Way estate in front of us and the Christopher Close area looking brand spanking new. The fair is all set out on the Village green though sheeted down which gives the impression that it might be Sunday.

The photograph above is the latest we have and clearly depicts the great changes in the size and layout of the village that have taken place since the beginning of the 1960s. Compare these photographs also with the colour picture taken in the early 1990s on the rear cover of the book.

Changes in Heckington during my lifetime
Laura Hulse
10th year Pupil at Kesteven & Sleaford High School.

I have lived in Heckington all my life and have noticed many changes, like new housing developments, changes in shops and services and population change. I also know of many other events in Heckington, like the opening of the bypass and the move of the primary school.

Heckington is a typical growing village. Changes in agriculture and subsequent intervention from the District Council Planning Authority have led to tremendous growth in recent years. In some ways Heckington is much the same as many villages in the East Midlands today with new red brick estates grafted onto the side of much smaller settlements.

The village lies midway between the towns of Sleaford and Boston in Lincolnshire and sits just off the A17 main road.
Population growth: 1981: 1,955, 1991: 2,124, 1998: 2,696, 2001: 3,000+.

The building boom started in the 1960s with small developments of 20+ houses (although these seemed large to the village at the time) to the estates of hundreds of houses now being built.

The estates were built in the following order: Churchill Way, Godson Avenue, Christopher Close, Millview, Pocklington Way, Stirling Court, Potesgrave Way, Bramley Way, Wellington close and then the massive new estates to the north of Sleaford road.

The Heckington Bypass was officially opened on 14th December 1982, it was the culmination of much dedicated work by the Heckington Bypass Action Group. They had battled for 11 years to divert the heavy traffic and make the village safer for its residents. The whole campaign began in February 1971 when a lorry crashed into a pensioner's cottage on the High Street. The Group began to collect data and opinions to support their plea for the building of a bypass.

Now the bypass is no longer a dream but a reality, Mrs Audrey Shepherd Chairman of the Action group said, 'Villagers no longer have their sleep interrupted by vibrations caused by heavy traffic.'

It is the general feeling of Heckington people that the village itself has 'come alive' since the opening of the bypass.

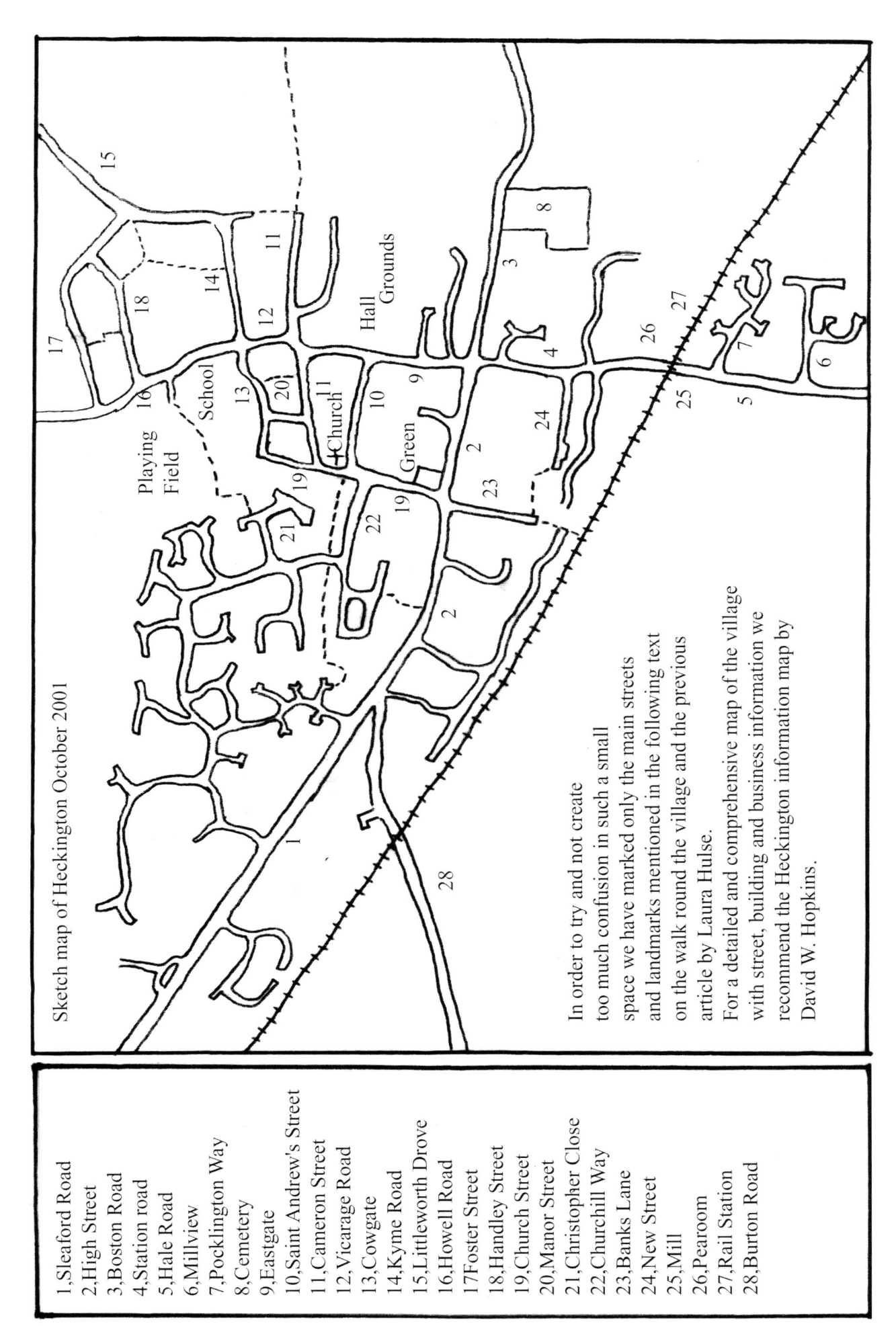

Sketch map of Heckington October 2001

In order to try and not create too much confusion in such a small space we have marked only the main streets and landmarks mentioned in the following text on the walk round the village and the previous article by Laura Hulse.
For a detailed and comprehensive map of the village with street, building and business information we recommend the Heckington information map by David W. Hopkins.

1. Sleaford Road
2. High Street
3. Boston Road
4. Station road
5. Hale Road
6. Millview
7. Pocklington Way
8. Cemetery
9. Eastgate
10. Saint Andrew's Street
11. Cameron Street
12. Vicarage Road
13. Cowgate
14. Kyme Road
15. Littleworth Drove
16. Howell Road
17. Foster Street
18. Handley Street
19. Church Street
20. Manor Street
21. Christopher Close
22. Churchill Way
23. Banks Lane
24. New Street
25. Mill
26. Pearoom
27. Rail Station
28. Burton Road

A WALK ROUND THE VILLAGE

A good way of understanding Heckington both old and new is to take a walk around the centre of the village. In particular we want to look at the streets in the area enclosed by Church Street, Cowgate, Kyme Road, Cameron Street, Eastgate, Station Road and back along the High Street. With occasional diversions this is the route we will follow to see some of the buildings that show the history of Heckington and to tell the stories of some of its intriguing characters from the past.

Starting at the village green, this piece of open ground at the centre of the village has probably remained as common land since Saxon times. The spot where the village crest now stands was the place where the first village pump was sunk in 1863 following a typhoid outbreak, in order to provide a convenient and safe water supply.

The sinking of the parish pump on the Village Green in 1863.
Photograph given to M.C.Sumners by Mr Neville Almond.

Among the houses, which benefited from this were the Almshouses on the north side of the green. One of the residents during the First World War was Grandma Lindsay. She would spend part of her precious five shillings a week pension on a daily newspaper and then read aloud the accounts of the progress of the war to the other ladies in the almshouses. On the wall was a picture of Garibaldi, the hero of Italian independence, and on the table under the lattice window a large family Bible. The floor of the cottage was made of red tiles covered with hand-made rugs. Every Saturday morning local children had to wash this floor, together with the red brick path outside, as part of their chores.

The Almshouses were originally built through a charity set up in 1720 by William Taylor. Poor William was dying at the time he established the charity so he put a note in his will asking his father to make sure that his bequest was honoured. The original buildings were thatched houses. They must have looked quaint, but thatch always suffers from the risk of fire and two of them burned down in 1833. The remaining two fell into disrepair until 1886 when another local benefactor, Henry Godson, had them all rebuilt as we see them today. They cost £750 to build and were left *"in trust for widows in necessitous circumstances"*. Henry Godson was also wealthy enough to have the flat roof on the church restored to the pitched roof we see today. So the view from the village green towards the almshouses and church was changed single-handedly by the generosity of this one man.

This photograph taken by M.C.Sumners in 1867 shows the remaining two almshouses when they were still in use and the Church roof half way through the restoration.

The only part of the picture, which Henry Godson did not create, is of course the red telephone box beside the Almshouses. It is at least likely to remain a part of the village landscape, since the telephone box is our smallest listed building. In fact we know from early reports that the telephone is not the first public utility to occupy this site. The village stocks used to stand close by as a punishment and deterrent to miscreants and vagabonds!

The new almshouses not long after they were built in 1886.

CHURCH STREET

The view down Church Street is still recognisable from early photographs. The post office on the corner, built in 1868, started life as one of Heckington's many butchers shops. The proof can be seen in the large door on the Church Street side, which was the entrance to the slaughterhouse. It was only in March 1902 when Michael Cole Sumners gave up the post office at his High Street chemists shop that Arthur Creasey decided there were too many butchers in Heckington and converted his shop into the new village post office.

This photograph taken in the early 1900s shows the large doors on the left to what was once the slaughterhouse in the post office and also the Universal Stores next door. The thatched building is the Six Bells.

The post office photographed at a much later date, probably in the 1940s. The trees on the Village Green have been re-planted behind the new iron railings. Just visible on the left is the bakers shop.

Further down Church Street is the Windmill Shop, so popular now for fruit and vegetables. The building dates from 1840 and has been a shop of one kind or another ever since. Perhaps its most distinctive incarnation was as Heckington's own "Universal Stores" in the 1920s. Beyond it was a saddlers and then a large thatched pub, the Six Bells, where Lindsay James and the hairdressers now stand. The Six Bells was typical of village pubs up until very recent times in that the landlords did not expect to make a living by selling beer alone. Part of it served as a hairdressers and part also as a tobacconists and newspaper shop. The papers used to arrive by train and were fetched each morning on a handbarrow from the station. The fate of the Six Bells is still remembered by Sandra Sardeson who, as a little girl in the 1950s, lived in Albion House three doors further down the street: *"I was sleeping in the back bedroom one night and woke up feeling very hot. My father told me to get up quickly and leave the house. As I rushed outside the street was lit up from a blazing fire in the thatch of the Six Bells. The sparks were flying all around and my father was very worried that they would set alight the petrol pump next door. The fire brigade sprayed water on that petrol tank all night and saved it from exploding, but they couldn't save the Six Bells and by the next morning it was no more than a smouldering heap of ashes."*

The Six Bells Inn with Curt's hairdressers, tobacconist & newsagents to the right.
To the left is the saddlers. It is possible that it is he who is posing with the postman.

Albion House, where Sandra lived, dates from about 1810 and was probably built as a farmhouse. Certainly it was a farm before the Second World War and was later owned by Jack Taylor the village schoolteacher. As well as academic studies he encouraged the local children to learn practical skills like digging and concrete making. The evidence was discovered by the current owner of the house who excavated a rockery in the back garden only to find a well proportioned concrete garden pond. Despite the ravages of time and weather, the pond held water as soon as it was filled, more than fifty years after the local children had created it for Mr Taylor as part of their surprisingly wide ranging school curriculum.

On the opposite side of the street was a row of cottages, now demolished and replaced by a single dwelling, although the shop on the corner of the green survives, distinguished by its large display window at the front. At one time it was an apothecary or chemists shop, though in living memory it has also been a jewellers, clothes shop, hairdressers and antiques shop.

Photograph taken by M.C.Sumners in 1860s showing cottages on the right with the corner shop. The Church still has a flat roof. On the left is the Six Bells and a magnificent barber's pole as well as all the hairdressing staff posing outside.

Despite these diversions, they must have been great meat eaters in former times since there was yet another butchers shop at the house beside the Methodist Chapel. The Chapel itself is built on the paddock where the butcher used to keep his animals before slaughter. Opposite this was a large three-storey Georgian House that was pulled down in the 1960s to open up the land for Churchill Way and the modern houses which spread out from it.

A view taken from the Church tower showing the paddock where the chapel was to be built. Also in the distance the War Memorial has yet to be constructed.

This was the large three storey Georgian house that was demolished to provide access for the Churchill Way development in the early sixties. It had been the home of the Godson family who had dominated village life for a century and a half. A well known and well liked family of local benefactors.

KILLING THE PIG

Despite all the butchers shops in the village, in the years around the second world war many families would still keep a pig of their own, feeding it on household scraps to fatten it up. When it was ready they would ask one of the local slaughtermen to come round and kill it. One of the last of these masters of the art was a man named Peg Reddish. He also built the former fish shop on Kyme Road. The sound of a pig squealing as its throat was cut was instantly recognisable to villagers up until quite recent times. The stuck pig was laid on a wooden frame or "cratch" and the women came out with buckets of very hot water to pour onto it. The water had to be just the right temperature to make the skin relax so its whiskers could be scraped off, without it being too hot to scald and discolour the skin. Later the carcase was hung on a wooden tripod or "cambril" for the meat to set before it was cut up. One lucky pig, not one of Peg Reddish's, is known to have escaped after its throat was cut and actually survived. The wound healed up and the pig lived wild down the fen, never again trusting human beings to come near enough to catch it.

The wife of one of the vicars created another piece of porcine history in the 1950s. She was a stalwart of local charity fund raising, but unfortunately not the best of cooks. She once made a cake and took it to the village hall for a Bring and Buy. The organiser, Mrs Starbuck, thanked her warmly but then quietly put the cake away under the table, rather than risk a complaint from a disgruntled buyer. As she was clearing up at the end, Mrs Starbuck remembered the cake, put a donation in the kitty and took it home to give to her pig. First thing next morning Mrs Starbuck was knocking on the door of George Knight the butcher. George was needed to come and butcher Mrs Starbuck's pig, which had mysteriously died during the night. So perhaps cake baked by the vicar's wife was really the last pig killer of Heckington!

THE WHITE HORSE AND THE MANOR HOUSE

Further down Church Street on the left is a former pub, the White Horse, which started life as a *"House of Industry"* or workhouse. A tablet on the wall commemorates its rebuilding in 1813 following a disastrous fire caused by an inmate smuggling a candle up to bed. The horror of being taken into the workhouse in old age still echoed in the memories of the elderly until at least the 1960s although Heckington's workhouse was converted to a pub in 1834 and is now a private house. A new workhouse was built in Sleaford to serve all the surrounding villages.

The old White Horse as it is today. The stone commemorating the workhouse fire can be seen above and to the left of the front door.

We now think of Church Street as a quiet residential centre, but apart from its former farms it also used to hum with the industry of a sawpit close to the corner with Cameron Street. This was where tree trunks were sawn by hand into planks using very long saws with handles on both ends. The sawyer would stand at the top end and the youngest apprentice had the handle at the lower end in the pit, where the sawdust must have been choking. Close by is Hope Cottage and beyond at right angles to the street is Toby Cottage, one of the last surviving *"mud and stud"* houses, which until the end of the 1800s, formed the majority of village residences.

Hope Cottage on the corner of Church Street and Cameron Street. A typical example of the D.G.Harris building design with the ornate gable end and the datestone of 1888. Two other trademarks common to many of his designs are the stained glass border to the upper sash window and the shape of the lower window.
Photographed in 2001 by K.Teasdale and digitally altered to represent the original building by P.Banister.

At the end of Church Street stands the Ferdowse clinic, formerly known as Heckington Manor. We have been able to trace the history of the site from earliest times, an account of which can be read elsewhere in this book. In the earliest reference to this area there was a mansion house called Boston Garth. A survival from medieval times to the present day is the name of the footpath from Cowgate to the playing field, Fishpond Lane. In living memory there was a large pond to the left of this path, which may well have dated back to the thirteenth or fourteenth century when fish were stored there to supplement the diet of the owners of the manor.

The Manor before the windows etc were altered

The core of the current house probably dates from the eighteenth century. In 1769 Richard Godson married Mary Taylor, heiress of the Taylor family who owned this site for over two hundred years, and it may well have been Richard and Mary who rebuilt the house after they moved to Heckington from Kirkby Laythorpe about 1780. Their son, the second Richard Godson and his teenage bride were certainly going to need a large house as they were to have at least eighteen and probably twenty children! Only eleven of these children survived to adulthood but several of them became great benefactors to the people of Heckington as will be seen by walking round the village.

Ernest Henry Godson, grandson of Richard and Elizabeth moved from Sleaford to the Heckington Manor with his wife and five daughters around 1900. Older residents of the village will have memories of the Miss Godsons who continued the family tradition of good works in the village. It was E.H.Godson who greatly remodelled and enlarged the house sometime before 1909 when the work was completed. A datestone is over the window in the 'new' extension.

The house remains much today as it was then. During the rebuilding some of the bay windows seen in the photograph on the preceding page were removed and reused at what is now the Vicarage, in Cameron Street, but was then the home of Mr Godson's unmarried sisters, Mary and Clara. An early case of recycling! Ernest H Godson was the founder of the firm of Solicitors still practising in Sleaford, and was greatly respected.

Ernest Henry Godson.

In June 1928 Ernest Godson, his wife and three of his daughters went on holiday to the Norwegian Fiords where Ernest died suddenly. His body was brought back to Newcastle on the SS Jupiter, conveyed by train to Grantham, and then by road back to Heckington for burial. Such was the impact of this sudden tragic death on the people of Heckington and the area that from the time the news of the death reached Sleaford until after the funeral the flag at the Sleaford Picturedrome was flying at half mast.

The Fishpond mentioned on preceding page, as it was up to the late fifties. It has since been filled in and is now part of the primary school nature area.

COWGATE

Turning now down Cowgate. At one time all the cottages here were built of mud and stud, mostly painted white and with thatched roofs, presenting a typical view of a Lincolnshire village. With the coming of the railway in the 1850s, the village began to grow and postal services also improved so they had to give names to the streets of the village for the first time. In the 1850s a local newspaper complained that, *"Heckington would be grand place if they would only decide on the street names."* Certainly the evidence of the 19th century suggests there were continual arguments over street names. One of the oldest of these names is Cowgate. It is rumoured that a member of the council saw local farmer Chunky Hardstaff walking his cow down the road and so the name was coined, although less romantic historians believe it was simply because Cowgate marked the edge of the village leading out into open pasture. Cowgate once extended into what we now know as "Kyme Road", but this was changed through common usage. The same was true of Howell Road, which once was called Vicarage Road. In the past Eastgate was called Copewall Street, while Cameron Street had an earlier existence as Chapman Street and at one time was confusingly known as St Andrews Street. Between Cameron Street and Cowgate is Goosegog Lane. The footpath sign mistakenly says Gooseberry Lane, conjuring images of a fruit-lined path. In fact it was a favourite place for local lads to kiss their girlfriends with friends stationed as lookouts or *"goosegogs"* at both ends of the lane.

This photograph of the Cowgate Vicarage Road corner was taken by M.C.Sumners just before the gasworks was built.

Further down Cowgate where the bungalow at number 22 now stands, Heckington's very own gasworks once stood at the corner with Vicarage Road on land owned by local doctor Moses Franks. It was funded by local subscriptions and built by the Heckington Gas Company in the early 1860s. The gas was generated from coal and was used for lighting rather than heating. The landlord of the Axe and Cleaver pub carted the coal from the station to the gasworks. On the return journey his cart was loaded with tar, a by-product of the gasworks. This is usually called coal tar, but in Heckington was always known as "gas tar". A curious reminder of this forgotten trade still exists. Just as the tar cart was about to turn into the station yard one of its wheels broke and the cartload of tar spilled onto what was then a dirt track Station Road. Instead of trying to salvage the tar, the quick-witted local residents spread out the tar as best they could to improve the road surface. Even now car drivers will still notice that the road rises and then falls steeply at the level crossing, as they go over the ramp left by that original load of tar.

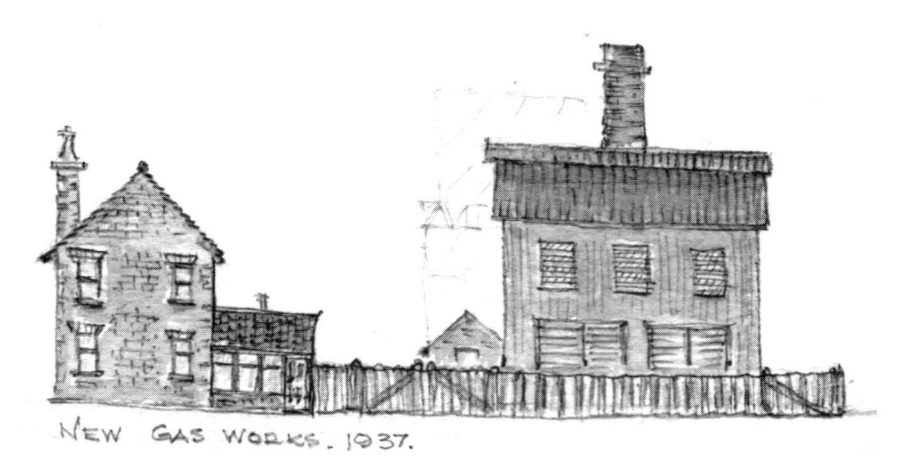

In the absence of a photograph of the gasworks we are grateful for this sketch by Richard Mowberry ARICS. MRSH. Chartered Surveyor Ret'd. However he stresses that it is from memory. There may have been variations over the years.

We tend to think of the village as largely residential but just one hundred years ago most of the streets had farms within them and adjacent farmland broke up the rows of houses. Only the central square between Church Street, St Andrews Street, Eastgate and the High Street was fully built up. Before the advent of the car, the village was virtually self sufficient not only in meat and produce but also in local trades. For example in Cowgate there was a wheelwright, joiner and undertaker. Where the new school now stands was once an orchard and market garden with a flat cart loaded with boxes leaving for market every Monday morning in season.

George Mowberry takes a break from the manufacture of a coffin at his workshop down Cowgate. The bungalow at number 11, now occupies the site.

KYME ROAD

Kyme Road was another centre of local industry. It used to be home to George Dodson, a man who was so keen on his bricklaying trade that his unfortunate neighbours used to have their sleep interrupted at 4am by the ringing of George's trowel as he lost no time in getting down to work. Walking down Kyme Road behind the houses on the left is Elm Holt.

Kyme Road and the Elm Holt before it was built on.

The area was once coppiced woodland. "Coppicing" means cutting trees right down to the ground every two years or so. This treatment produces lots of new branches that grow up straight as poles and can be used for fencing, making the staves of wheels or the legs of chairs. However, Elm Holt also had its leisure uses and was for many years a favourite recreation ground for village children as well as a meeting place for courting couples. The woods at one time came right up to Kyme Road and stretched back to what is now Foster Street. We know building along Kyme Road commenced soon after the First World War and began to eat into Elm Holt around 1926. That was the year Haverholme Priory near Ewerby was demolished and two houses on Kyme Road, Priory Holme and Nine Elms, incorporate features such as windows, doors, and fireplaces that were bought at auction when Haverholme was gutted.

The Elm Holt in a more leisurly time.

FROM BUGGY BELL'S LANE TO CAMERON STREET

Beyond Elm Holt, at the point where Kyme Road bends to the left, if you are on foot you can turn right into Buggy Bell's Lane and head back to Cameron Street. Buggy Bell was a cobbler who had a workshop here in the early 1900s. His lane returns to Cameron Street at the point where a footpath leads out across fields. This footpath probably represents an ancient route leading out into the fens from the centre of the village and may date back to Roman times since it leads towards the Roman tile kiln on the Car Dyke. All the older houses at this end of Cameron Street used to belong to Hall Farm and were built for farm workers on the estate.

The house on the corner of Hall Close was built by a wealthy 19th Century owner of Heckington Hall, William Little, for his personal manservant and was later used to house his gardener. The modern Hall Close used to be the rear entrance to Heckington Hall and opened into the stable yard, greenhouses, potting sheds and orchard.

View looking down Cameron Street to the east from Vicarage road corner. The house built for William Little's manservant, later to be used by the gardener, can be seen to the right, together with the large wooden gates that were the rear entrance to the Hall.

Like so many other streets in the village, Cameron Street was not only a place of residence but also a hive of activity, housing coal merchants, a wheelwright and several farmyards. The Axe and Cleaver pub was on the corner of Vicarage Road and Cameron Street, next to what is now Knight's Butchers. In 1864 the Axe and Cleaver was rebuilt, functioning as a mixed pub, farm, and butchers. Only men went to the pubs in those days and the toilet was a one standing urinal at the far end of the yard. Since the pub was also a working farm, those who were a little unsteady on their feet stood a very real risk of tripping over a harrow or plough as they made their way across the yard.

Looking up Vicarage Road on a cold winter's day many years ago with the Axe and Cleaver to the right. The large barn can be clearly seen and next to that along the road is the rather smaller building which is the butcher's shop.

The corner of Vicarage Road by the old school is now an open grassy area dominated by fine silver birch trees, planted in the *"year of the tree"* 1973. However this sweeping corner was only created in the late 1950s when several dilapidated cottages that lined the roadside were pulled down. One former inhabitant of these cottages, Mr Mann, was always known as *"dilly Mann"*. A *"dilly cart"* is a Lincolnshire term for an open horse-drawn cart that collected night soil in the days before a proper sewer system was available.

Older villagers can still recall dilly Mann, his foul-smelling cart slowly crawling up the High Street of an evening. He would pull up outside the fish shop, carefully wiping his hands on his trousers before buying his fish and chips, which he then ate from the newspaper wrapping as he headed back home in his cart.

The old school corner as it was before the cottages where Mr Mann lived were demolished in the early sixties. Photograph taken by Mrs Irene Zealand.

In the schoolyard near the junction of Cameron Street and Eastgate was the schoolmaster's house which later became the caretaker's house. One of its most celebrated occupants was Miss Cooper, a single woman who was the school caretaker and lived there during the Second World War and who died in the 1950s. She used to foster as many as six orphaned or homeless children at a time. The headmaster's notes of the period say that, *"Miss Cooper is behind with the rent. She has promised to pay because she has taken in extra needlework"*. The indefatigable Miss Cooper also cleaned the school and some former pupils can still remember her coming in to the classroom before PE with a bucket of damp sand that was swept over the floor to clean it.

The schoolhouse and school in the early 1900s. The school bell known as the 'pancake bell' and hung in the gable end tower was blown down in a gale the 1970s.
The last sawpit to be used in the village was down a drive to the left of the house in the 1920s.

The photograph above is of Miss Cooper when she was a young woman.
The group to the right are some of the children who were brought up by her in the 1920s.
From left to right they are; Ethel, Kathy Mac Dougal, Dolly, Rene and Doris.

Across the road from the school in Cameron Street is a house with a shop front. In the late 19th Century it was Ben Levesley's shop, an important source of fashionable clothing for the better-off villagers of the day. Instead of buying in their stock, they had fashion plates from Paris and teams of up to 18 seamstresses who made the clothes to order. They must have been very good, as even the Countess of Winchilsea is known to have patronised Levesley's. The Chapmans had a large and flourishing drapers, grocers and bakers business close by. They were important villagers in the 1880s, as evidenced by the presentation in January 1887 to Mr Chapman of a silver tea and cream ewer on his 80th birthday *"as a testimony of respect by his fellow parishioners."* At one stage, in typical Heckington fashion, Cameron Street was even named *"Chapman Street"*. Perhaps one reason the Chapmans were so popular was because their baker's business was useful for rather more than baking bread. On their way to church on Sunday, well-organised villagers would drop off their joints of meat to have them put into the large ovens of the bake house so that they could take them home after church, ready-cooked.

The Vicarage in Cameron Street, named after the Reverend Cameron who served the parish between 1861-1894. The home of the Reverend David Boutle in the year 2001. Photo by K.Teasdale.

Beyond Chapman's is the modern vicarage, although it took a long time for the vicars of Heckington to move so close to the church. From medieval times the vicarage was out in the fen towards South Kyme. It was only in the 19th century that they moved to a vicarage in what is now Howell Road. The current vicarage in Cameron Street used to be called "Church Side" and at one time was a farmhouse. Mary and Clara Godson moved there in the early 1900s. Mary and Clara were born in the 1860s and died within a year of each other in 1946 and 1947. They were the spinster sisters of the wealthy owner of Heckington Manor, Ernest Henry Godson. When he carried out an extensive remodelling of the Manor he also refurbished Church Side for his sisters, fitting bay windows that were re-used from the Manor. The Miss Godsons were village benefactors, running Heckington's first lending library in the village hall. Mary and Clara Godson moved out of Church Side in the early 1950s when the diocese bought it for the Reverend Skelton in 1952 and so, probably for the first time since the middle ages, the vicarage was once more established next to the church.

Drawing of the Reverend G.T.Cameron MA taken from the book Heckington in the 1870s previously published by the Village Trust.
He created such a lasting impression on the people of the village that Cameron Street was named after him. He founded a branch of the Church of England Temperance Society, was chairman of the Church Missionary society and the British and Foreign bible Society. He also worked hard with various other community benefactors for the relief of the poor.

This photograph of the old Red Cow Inn was taken just before it was demolished to make way for the smart red brick building that still stands to this day. It was taken from the Churchyard by Michael Cole Sumners on what looks to have been a particularly bleak winter's day.

Opposite the Church there used to be yet another pub, the Red Cow, that was rebuilt in 1897. It incorporated a butcher's shop, which flourishes today as Turnells. During the war, the Red Cow was well known for its dances, held in the big room at the back of the butcher's. Meanwhile in the bar at the front of the building the regular drinkers looked out on the churchyard with its yews, gravestones and ghosts, of which they used to say, *"The more you drank, the more yew saw"*.

The new Red Cow probably not long after it was built as the Godson Almshouses have yet to be constructed on the opposite corner. Note the public standpipe on the roadside for fresh water.

THE CHURCHYARD

The monuments in the churchyard can tell other more genuine stories of village life. Among them is the tombstone to Charles Cameron. He was invited to preach in the church at his brother George's inauguration as vicar of Heckington. Sadly the service did not go to plan. Charles' tombstone recalls that he received his summons on that Advent Sunday in 1861 at the age of 54, while preaching from the pulpit. Another death is recorded on the faded and weathered tombstone near the vestry door, to an ex-sailor. He was lodging in Heckington, possibly on leave. He called in at one of the village beer houses and had a long session gambling at cards with 3 others. His gravestone reads:

'In memory of William Orton Burbank late of Whissendine in the county of Rutland and formerly a seaman on board HMS the Centaur who was inhumanly murdered the 9th day of March 1833 on the Turnpike Road within one and a half miles of the Town. Aged 45 years.' His murderer, 21 years old William Taylor of Heckington was hanged 9 days later at Lincoln Castle.

Presumably the parish paid for the sailor's gravestone, but at least one Heckington resident went to the trouble of not just of paying for a monument but also building it for himself in the village cemetery on Boston Road. The man in question was an early Heckington developer named Daniel Gorham Harris. If you want to know how he made his money and reputation then look about the village for houses with square datestones prominent on them, all coming from the late 19th and early 20th century. Harris loved to put datestones on his work, which includes the row of cottages in St Andrews Street, Hope Cottage on the corner of Church Street and Cameron Street, and Diamond Jubilee Terrace opposite the Post Office. There are plenty more besides. Harris was a self made man. He was born in 1841 but his father died in an accident when he was only seven years old, so he had to go out to service. We know he came to Heckington as a footman to the vicar, George Cameron, in 1861. Eleven years after this, Harris commenced business as a grocer and draper with a shop in St Andrews Street. The shop earned him enough money to begin house building as the village started to grow in the wake of the arrival of the railway. He himself lived in St Andrews Villa and also owned the Harris Press, which stood in the grounds of the house.

Diamond Jubilee Terrace on the left. Built by D.G.Harris in 1897.

Harris seems to have been a religious man, but he had his ups and downs with the established church. In the 1880s he was choirmaster of Heckington Church and always announced the hymns. However, one day the vicar decided that he was going to announce the hymns himself and duly took over in the middle of a service. This was more than Harris was prepared to tolerate.

"*Let's strike boys*", he is recorded as saying and the whole orchestra stood up there and then and carried their instruments out of the church. He is buried in Heckington cemetery with a suitably imposing monument.

Saint Andrews Terrace as it is today with its trademark Harris datestone. Photo by P.Banister.

SAINT ANDREWS STREET

Leaving the churchyard, straight in front of you in St Andrews Street is Church House. It was built in 1835 and started life as the second Wesleyan Chapel in the village, reputed to be able to seat 290 people, which must have been a squash. It became redundant in 1905 when the much larger chapel in Church Street was built. It was bought by the Godson family and became a public reading room for people to read the newspapers and the Bible, and was then donated to the church, so that it is now known as St Andrews Centre.

The Saint Andrews Centre with its modern access ramps and guard rails in the foreground and the old police house now a private residence, next to it in the background. Photographed in 1999 by Pat Banister.

If you look behind the St Andrews Centre, you will see a faded pink lean-to building. This once housed the village fire engine. The engine started life as a horse drawn contraption that at one stage was kept in the church. During the Second World War it was upgraded to a petrol driven engine and run by the Auxiliary Fire Service team. After the War the fire engine seems to have disappeared, so its pink garage remains empty.

The wartime firemen above were, from left to right on the back row;
G.Wolds, J.Asher, G.Hewardine, J.Hall, V.Stevenson, E.Miller, J.Marshall, J.Tear.
Front row from left to right;
W.Line, J.Lowth, F.Scoggins, W.Ward, J.Woods, S.Rudkin.

Just to the right is the former police station that was built about 1840 and has now been converted to a house. It must have been one of the earliest village police stations in the county. If you look at the front of the building it is easy to imagine a blue lamp outside the steps that lead up to the front door. The lock-up cells still survive inside. The village must have been an unruly place in the 1840s as the police station housed both a sergeant and a constable. It was eventually replaced by a police house in Burton Road and now the new building next to the Surgery on Sleaford Road.

The new police offices next to the surgery on the Sleaford Road. The photograph was taken in 1999 by Mary Wilkinson and shows PC Powell closing down the station on his final day as the last local village bobby.

Continuing the walk around the village, if you go down St Andrews Street towards Eastgate, beyond the high brick wall on your right is a stone house which may have been constructed out of the medieval tithe barn that still stood in this part of the village in the 1500s, perhaps beside a now lost path leading to the High Street. Further down St Andrews Street, where the bungalows now stand on the left hand side, used to be Bowden's shop, selling sweets, bread, and cakes. Mrs Bowden is remembered as the organist at the Methodist chapel.

This old house stands back from the road and at right angles to the Church on Saint Andrews Street. The photograph taken by M.C.Sumners shows a little girl of nine who grew up to be Doll Sumners, the last of the family to own the chemists shop on the High Street. A path led through the garden to the shop from here.

EASTGATE

The redbrick house at the corner of St Andrews and Eastgate used to be a shop and beside it on Eastgate stands St Andrew's Terrace, displaying yet another of DG Harris' stone plaques. Maggie Hall had a little sweet shop in this terrace up until the 1980s, full of large jars of penny sweets even then. On the left hand side of the exit from St Andrews Street into Eastgate is a building now divided into three dwellings. It was once a single large house with the last of the old thatched roofs left in the village until it was replaced with a modern roof in the 1970s. Although not obvious from the outside, this is in fact a timber-framed house, perhaps dating from the 15th century. Beside it is a more modern addition, the Wesleyan Reform Chapel that was built in the 1850s.

The Wesleyan Reform Chapel built of local brick in 1858. The row of houses in the distance are the timber framed building mentioned above.
Photographed in 1999 by P.Banister.

Opposite is Heckington Hall, once known as Hall Farm. It is a late 17th century house, re-cased in the 19th century. Its most famous owner was William Little who bought it in 1862, together with the 330-acre farm, for the princely sum of £19,050. William Little was in partnership with the Boston MP Herbert Ingram and together in 1842 they founded the Illustrated London News. Eventually, having made his fortune, William Little decided to move away from London. Heckington was the obvious choice as he had married Elizabeth Godson and the advent of the railway meant he could continue to visit the capital while also enjoying rural life. Little had originally trained as a chemist at the Sorbonne and during his time in Heckington he invented "Little's Dip", a patent sheep dip. It was William and Elizabeth Little who first allowed the Hall grounds to be used for the Heckington Show. William's unpublished diary records the event: *"30th July 1867: Flower show, organ opening. A tolerably fine day. The flower show held in the Rookery. Many visitors and a great success."* In later years they would have dancing on the lawn by the Hall on Show evenings and shortly after the gasworks opened they installed special gas lights to illuminate the dancing. The Show usually ended with a firework display and the last of the firework set pieces always said, *"Thank you Mrs Little"*.

Some scenes of great merriment in the grounds of Mr Littles house. Possibly the celebrations for King George V silver jubilee.

Moving up from the Hall towards the High Street, Cobham Close was built in the 1980s on the site of Hall Farm yard, marking the end of the last working farmyard in the centre of the village. Close by on the opposite side there is a plaque on a wall which marks the site of the Chapel of the Particular Baptists. One of the village families associated with them was the Nash family, who were millers and owned the windmill at the Station until 1890. At that time Eastgate comprised mainly little cottages and crowded yards, many of which were very unsanitary. The courtyards would all have had wells for drinking water, but the yards also contained chicken runs usually with a pigsty at one side, with the result that disease was rife. The conditions gave much concern to the rural sanitary authority inspector from Sleaford. One of the worst incidents was where a pigsty adjoined a neighbouring cottage and the hungry pig actually broke its way through the adjoining wall and into the house. At least the problem of the poor water supply was resolved in 1894 when a village water tower was built on Sleaford Road and stand pipes with clean water were set up in all the main streets of the village. Rumour has it that William Little and Ernest Godson were at first against the building of the water tower, until it was agreed that the height of the tower should be raised sufficient to deliver running water into their own tanks in both the Manor and the Hall.

Looking down Eastgate from the cross roads with the row of old cottages on the left. On the right just beyond the house is where the council chambers would be built.

The children congregate in Eastgate outside Granny Brown's fish and chip shop on the left.
On the right is another public standpipe for the suppy of fresh water.

Sleaford Road with the water tower in the distance. The state of the road shows that horses were still the main form of transport then.

The demolition of the water tower in the mid 60s. Photographed by A.Line.

Datestone for Baptist Chapel in Eastgate, 1896.

The Little's estate sold the parish council the land in Eastgate, on which the current council chamber was built, for £7. 10s in 1931. It was built by local firm Porters at a cost of £144. 15s and first used on 15th September 1931. When the first parish council was formed in 1894 there were 11 places to fill. The Conservatives and the Liberals were the rival political parties of the day. They both met on the same night, the Conservatives in the schoolroom and the Liberals in the Temperance Hall. They quickly chose five candidates each, but could not agree on the extra one. After a great deal of running between the two by messenger, they managed to avoid a parish council election by drawing lots for the final seat, with the Conservatives winning the extra seat. The local paper, with scant regard for democracy, recorded that with a village of about 1,800 inhabitants it was an honour to them all that such an arrangement had been made and an election avoided.

The council chambers in Eastgate. Now also the parish office. The original gas light fittings are still intact although not in use. Photograph by K.Teasdale. Digital enhancement by P.Banister.

BOSTON ROAD

Until the opening of the bypass in 1982 this was part of the busy main road from the midlands to Norfolk. At the corner of Eastgate and Boston Road stands The Royal Oak. This used to be an old building at the roadside before it was demolished and rebuilt in its present position.

The Royal Oak as it was in years gone by. This is probably not the first pub to occupy the site. There is talk of a mud and stud building before this one.

It was an important coaching inn during the early 1800s when the Newark to Kings Lynn stagecoach would always stop at the Royal Oak. Further up Boston Road on the same side as the Oak is Heckington House, a fine family house that is remembered as an officers' mess during the Second World War. Apparently they used to do weapons practice there and local children recall picking up live rounds in the yard as souvenirs!

Heckington House on the right, photographed from the cemetery a good many years ago when the two giant Wellingtonia redwood trees stood either side of the gates. One of them can be seen on the left of the picture.

Further along and on the opposite side is the cemetery. This was built from a design submitted by Richard Almond, Architect of Palace Chambers Westminster and approved on 5th April 1879. In those days the various churches in the village seem to have been less willing to co-operate than now. So the cemetery was built with not one, but two chapels. One was Anglican, facing east, and one Nonconformist, facing west, separated by an archway.
The eastern chapel has recently been refurbished and is open daily as a place for quiet meditation.

The cemetery chapels minus the bell which was discovered to be badly cracked and has been removed by the parish council for recasting.
Photographed by Pat Banister

The cemetery was administered by a burial board of nine ratepayers elected under the chairmanship of the vicar Reverend Cameron, who is rumoured finally to have dropped his opposition to the new cemetery only when it was agreed that he could receive all the burial fees. Coming back towards the village is Wellington House where Major Lawrence used to live and served as chairman of the Show for 20 years. The once fine gardens of the house now form the new residential development of Wellington Close.

Wellington House viewed from the air in the early sixties, long before thoughts of developing the gardens for housing. At this time it was the home of the school headmaster Mr Woods, his schoolteacher wife and their family.

THE MILL / STATION COMPLEX

Turning down Station Road is Heckington's famous windmill. It is the only surviving example of an eight-sail windmill in Britain. It was actually built as a five-sail mill in 1830 by Edward Ingledew of Gainsborough for its new owner, the 25-year old Michael Hare. Sadly Michael died within a few years leaving his wife Anne a widow of twenty-nine. However she did not remain a widow for very long, choosing instead to marry a sixty-five year old baker, Sleightholme Nash, whose family retained the mill for much of the 19th century. However, in 1890 when the mill workers were having a lunchtime drink at the nearby Railway Hotel a sudden storm arose. The top of the mill was blown off and a fire started, gutting the tower. The mill might easily have been demolished had it not been for the opportunist purchase by John Pocklington of removable parts from an eight-sail mill at Skirbeck near Boston at about the same time. One of his modern descendants, Ron Pocklington, takes up the tale:

One Wednesday in 1891 Mr Nash was at Boston Market and saw Mr Pocklington. He asked him what he intended to do with the mill machinery he had just bought and Mr Pocklington replied that he had no idea. Mr Nash soon said that there was an empty tower at Heckington for sale and Mr Pocklington was sufficiently interested to take the 6 o'clock train with him to view it. He bought it with its bakehouse and the small parcel of land for £250."

The Pocklington family maintained their new mill until the Second World War, when it ceased to be active and the shutters were removed. In 1953 it was bought by Kesteven County Council and then gradually renovated by local effort as an important modern tourist attraction.

Photograph by P. Banister 1999

The area around the mill changed suddenly in 1858 with the coming of the Boston, Sleaford and Midland Counties railway. The Station was typical of hundreds of similar country stations, which revolutionised the lives of local people by making it possible for them to travel far and wide and to trade their produce in city markets. Trains continue to stop at Heckington en route to Grantham, Nottingham, Boston and Skegness. The station buildings have been saved by the Village Trust and now house a railway museum. The Signal Box is also 19th century and retains many of its original fittings.

The nineteenth century signal box with the now 'old fashioned' crossing gates. Photographed by Pat Banister.

Just an example of the tremendous number of artefacts on display at the railway museum complete with Stationmaster's desk. Photograph by P. Banister 2001.

Close by stands the Pearoom. This was built in 1870 and leased to the seed firm of Charles Sharpe of Sleaford. Sharpe's used it as a pea-sorting warehouse up until 1961. Locally grown peas were brought in by horse and cart but peas from further afield were delivered by rail for sorting and then exporting. During the depression of the 1930s the Pearoom provided work for many village women, often as the main source of income for the family. In the 1970s, again with leadership from the Heckington Village Trust, the Pearoom was converted into a heritage and craft centre. At this time it is managed under licence from The Trust by North Kesteven District Council.

The Pearoom in its heyday with horses moving the waggons in the railway sidings right up to the front doors.

This photograph take at the beginning of restoration work by the Village Trust shows the state to which the building had fallen and gives an idea of the task ahead of them through the 1970s.

Across the road stands the former Railway Hotel, built around 1860 by Robert Taylor. As well as providing refreshments for weary travellers, he operated a cattle cake and coal merchants business. Many of his papers and accounts still survive, showing that he used to handle up to £400 worth of cattle cake and 220 tons of coal a month, all of it brought in by rail. The large rooms in the purpose-built hotel were popular for meetings of village organisations such as the Society for the Prosecution of Felons, the Heckington Foal Show Society and the South Lincolnshire Artificial Manure Association, under its inventive patron Mr William Little of Heckington Hall. In sharp contrast, the Pig Club used to meet in that more working class pub, the Axe and Cleaver.

The Railway Hotel at the time when the whole station area was a hive of industry and commerce.

An Original Pig Club membership payment card from the 1950s kindly loaned to the group by Len Coulson of Cowgate.

Returning up Station Road towards the High Street is the site of a new residential development called Millers Way. However, new residents may be interested to know that its original name is "Butt's Hill Field", meaning the place where villagers practised archery in medieval times. It is named after the archery "*butts*", which were earth mounds that were used to prop up the targets and halt any errant arrows. In fact the archers of Heckington had more sense than to dig out a new mound for themselves. An archaeological excavation in 1815 revealed that they had simply used a round barrow dating from much earlier times.

Continuing towards the village is New Street. This was built by former mill owner John Pocklington. During a bout of depression, Pocklington was committed to an asylum by the village doctor. John never forgave the doctor for this and after his recovery is rumoured to have built the row of houses in New Street quite deliberately, in order to spoil the view from the doctor's garden. At the end of New Street is a footpath to Banks Lane, named after the family who were the last residents of the Old Hall, on the site where Diamond Jubilee Terrace now stands.

New Street looking east from the footpath which connects it to Banks Lane and the High Street. Photograph taken in 1999 by Pat Banister.

This shot of the old Hall by M.C.Sumners. shows evidence of the long exposures needed with early photography as the 'ghost' of a dog can be seen in the bottom right of the picture.

The blacksmith's (Cook's Corner) in days gone by. *From left to right;* Walter Lowth (smith & farrier), Walter Cook Snr, unknown apprentice, Frank Cook as a child, (elder brother of Walter), and Grandfather Billy Cook.

COOK'S CORNER AND THE HIGH STREET

Returning to Station Road and then to the High Street, the turning is known to villagers as "Cook's Corner" after the family that used to run the blacksmith's shop. However, their real source of fame is not horseshoes but elephants' shoes! The story is that a travelling circus once stopped there to seek help for a lame elephant and the Cooks skilfully obliged. The business is still thriving, now owned by village man Nick Marshall who makes and repairs farm machinery and other equipment.

On the left is Billy Cook and on the right wearing the trilby is Walter Cook senior. The photograph was taken in the 1920s in what, approximately, is now the garden of 12 Station Road where all of the wheel shoeing was carried out.

GEO. COOK,
HECKINGTON,
Shoeing & Jobbing Smith.

AGRICULTURAL IMPLEMENT MANUFACTURER.
All kinds of Reaping Machines repaired.
Tomb and Ornamental Railings made to order.
Agent for all the Best Makes of Implements, including Reapers, Ploughs &c.

Further down the High Street stands the Village Hall. It was built in 1858 and the plaque on the front shows that it started life as a Temperance Hall, a meeting place for the teetotal movement in the 19th century. The man who built it was Dr Moses Franks. He was the village doctor and became convinced that many of the health and social problems of his day were drink-related.

The Village Hall as it is today. The stone plaque on the wall above the front entrance tells of its origins. Photograph by M.Wilkinson 1999.

135

Franks started a temperance meeting group in one of the local chapels, but then became very annoyed when he was told the group could no longer go on meeting there, because they were not serving a religious function. Undaunted and with the confidence of the Victorian era, Dr Franks simply had a new hall built in his own front garden and at his own expense of £800. His efforts were derided in the local press as an unnecessary waste of money but the community as a whole has reason to be very grateful for his generosity in giving the Hall to the village when he retired in 1863. The central Hall was built with a caretaker's cottage on one side and a small two-storey section on the other side, which once housed the penny library. It cost a penny a month to join and this allowed you to borrow one book at a time. The Hall was further extended in 1920 and was used as the Picture Palace or cinema. There were three shows a week plus a Saturday Matinee for children. The building remained a temperance hall until the late 1960s when a new constitution finally permitted the sale of intoxicating liquor.

An early photograph of the Hall in the days of Dr Moses Franks and the temperance movement.

Just opposite is Latimer House, named after Thorpe Latimer where its original occupants, the Tomlinsons, came from. It was a stone house recased in its present form in the early 1900s. It used to be famed for its fine gardens. They were romantically extended by one of the 20th century owners of the house, Phil Hubbard. He bought up some small houses backing on to his property in St Andrews Street and then knocked them all down. The reason was so that his wife could walk from Latimer House to go to church on Sundays entirely through her own garden! Local girl Jenny Teasdale remembers Mr Hubbard as a kindly man. As an eight year-old she used to slip over the wall of her back garden in Eastgate to play in the Latimer House orchard. One day Mr Hubbard caught her in the orchard. He warned her against climbing the trees but told her she was welcome to come and play there any time.

Latimer House photographed by M.C.Sumners as it was in 1906.

The High Street has always been the centre for the village shops, even if the goods sold have changed considerably in recent years. For over a century the current pet shop was a tailors shop owned by Kirtons. Many village men were married in suits made to measure by Kirtons.

A very early photograph of Kirtons shop, just past the horse & trap together with the shop that preceded Almond's bus business.

The building presently occupied by Harvest Insurance has an association with travel and engineering. In the early 1900s it was a bicycle shop run by the Almond family. This then developed into a bus and taxi service.

137

The proud driver poses with the most up to date public transport of the time.

The business was subsequently taken over by Sharpe's who developed it further into car repairs and petrol sales with delivery pumps on the pavement. It even used to be Heckington's *"power station"*. A diesel generator was installed in the 1920s and this was used to charge up, amongst other things, the primitive radio batteries of the day. These were known as accumulators and people from far and wide could be seen bringing the in for recharging. Wires were soon strung up to supply neighbouring houses with power, even across the street.

One building in the High Street that has scarcely changed is Lloyds Bank. It has been a bank for 150 years since it first opened as a branch of Peacock and Handley's Bank. Another notable building is The Stone House, number 24, which probably dates from the late 17th century and is thought to have been built from stone from Cobham Hall. The Stone House was famously the home of Samuel Jessop, who by the time of his death in 1817 had established the world record for pill taking. According to the Guiness book of records, he took 226,934 pills over twenty one years between 1791 and 1816. In 1814 he swallowed 51,590 or about 140 every day. This, together with 40,000 bottles of medicine, kept him going to the age of 65.

Lloyds Bank photographed in 1999 by Mary Wilkinson. Barclays also had a bank on the opposite side of the road until a few years ago, at the house with the mosaic panel to the front.

On the left the Stone House, one time home of Samuel Jessop the prolific pill taker. In the centre of the photo is Latimer House after being revamped in about 1902.

Next door to the Stone House was the house and chemist's shop of Michael Cole Sumners. Mr Sumners began visiting Heckington in about 1860 from his home in Folkingham. It was at this time that he began taking photographs. He eventualy moved to the village in 1864 and thus began his love affair with photographing the village. Without him and his glass plate camera we would have nothing like the record of the village that is now at our disposal.

Pharmaceutical chemist and photographer Michael Cole Sumners at the door of his High Street premises when it was still also the post office. The post box can be seen to the right under the front window.

On the edge of the Green is the Nags Head pub. In the gable end is a datestone, *IH Ireland 1684.* The Irelands were known as coopers or barrel makers but in his inventory Henry Ireland is recorded as having owned a brewhouse with "*ten little flagons and quarts*", suggesting that his new building served as a tavern even in the 17th century. In 1733 the registry of ale houses shows Anne Clark as the inn-keeper and it was probably in her time or that of her sons that the Nags Head was extended to its current three storey height.

Detail of datestone on the gable end.

The Nag's Head when it boasted petrol pumps & tearooms as well as being an AA & RAC garage and an hotel with car park.

Opposite the Post Office is Diamond Jubilee Terrace, dating from 1897. It was built on the site of Heckington Hall, one of the village's grandest Georgian houses that featured its own carriageway. The last occupants of the Hall were the Banks family, hence the name of *"Banks Lane"* for the street that runs alongside. In Victorian times both Heckington Hall and the Red House, which still stands, were run as private boarding schools One of the gate piers from the Hall survives on the boundary with the Red House at 63 High Street.

SLEAFORD ROAD THEN BACK TO THE VILLAGE GREEN
Opposite the Red House, Crown Lodge records the site of another pub.

On the right is the Crown Inn on Sleaford Road photographed from the Red House gates. Opposite can be seen one of the then many petrol stations and the entrance to the smallholding site mentioned below.

On our walk around the village we have seen that for most of its history the centre of village contained working farms and smallholdings. The last smallholding to go was on the site developed as Shrubwood Close in the early 1990s. The name records the Shrubwood Nurseries where flowers, fresh fruit and vegetables were grown and sold in a shop on the site of Barn Cottage so you knew exactly where the produce had come from.

Another lost village amenity is remembered in Cobbler's Cottage, the site of Thorlby's shoe repair shop.

Moving further towards Sleaford, 62 High Street is a superb example of a village centre farmhouse, built from the profits of the enclosure of the open fields in the 18th century. Its best-remembered inhabitant is Pell Dickinson, the village poet, who lived there about fifty years ago. One of his poems remembers "*Yellow Hammer Lane*", which led southward off the High Street to Cottage Farm. The route has now been diverted and with a tarmac surface survives as "Lime Tree Walk".

The corner of Burton Road, High Street and Sleaford Road was always very wet, with ponds south of the High Street and in the angle between Burton Road and Sleaford Road. This served for watering stock and the washing of wagonwheels. In later years it also served as a stopping place for steam driven road traction engines, which would top up with water there. Perhaps this was also the reason why this site was chosen for the village water tower when piped water was introduced into the village in 1894-5.

This photograph shows the village pond mentioned above and also the Inkpot house (on the right) mentioned below.
In the distance can be seen one of the windmills also mentioned in the following article.

This western end of the village was traditionally the site for the village windmills, since they faced the prevailing wind. Mowberry's Mill still stands without its sails and there was once another mill opposite. These were built in the late 18th century, but "*ancient mills*" were first recorded in this area of the village in 1310 on the site of Millfield Farm.

Moving back towards the village centre, Potesgrave Way is another recently developed farmyard. At this point once stood the "*Inkpot House*", a charming little cottage which served as the gatehouse for a private road running to the Manor and owned by the Godson family.

Mowberry's mill as it was in its heyday. Parts of the sails remained up to the 1950s but today it's a hollow shell. One wonders if it could someday be restored to working order?

In the 19th century the Godsons owned much of the north side of Sleaford Road, including another windmill which stood on the site of Woodmans Park. Built at the end of the 18th century, it burnt down in 1894 when the flue from its auxiliary steam engine overheated. Part of the reason for its loss was the fact that water had to be pumped from the pond in Burton Road. The distance meant that it took two fire engines to pump the water along Sleaford Road and only one could actually fight the fire. The mill was demolished, but the engine house was converted into a residence for the Scoggins family, who set up a thriving woodworking business, even making farm waggons.

An easily missed feature of Sleaford Road is the Pinfold. It is now a charming walled garden but it was build in the 18th century as a parish repository for lost sheep and cattle, so they could be contained there until claimed by their owners. Once the sheep and cattle were banished from the centre of the village it was neglected and served only as a dump for road building materials. But village efforts saved and restored it in 1976, to create the pleasant garden we know today. Perhaps it was all that manure that makes the plants grow so well!

A look through the gate into the Pinfold, the ancient brickwork enhanced by the planting of herbs and flowers and looked after by the Gardening Club. Photographed in 1998 by Pat Banister.

Walking past Inge's restaurant which used to be a bakers and confectioners, and crossing the corner carefully by the Post Office brings us back to the Green and the War Memorial, built from Cornish granite in 1920 by public subscription. An idea in use by the Parish Council is to remember some of the local people on the memorial by naming new roads and footpaths after them. It seems a good way of keeping their memory alive, just as we have tried to do with some of the many characters recorded in this brief walk around our village.

Fresh flowers are placed on the War Memorial all year round.

A JOURNEY THROUGH TIME

Heckington in the past has been largely self-sufficient, self-supporting and self-governing. The slow pace of change has helped to create a village with strong ties of family and friendship and, occasionally, with equally great hostilities. It is clear from what we have described in earlier chapters that things have never remained the same in the village. But when changes are gradual they give people a better opportunity to adjust. There is also a difference between change which is imposed from outside and change which we can control for ourselves. One important feature of Heckington's history is that even major changes, such as the building of the railway or the establishment of the gas works, were instigated and funded by local people who exercised control over what was happening.

We cannot turn the clock back, even if we wanted to do so, and the pace of change is increasing with each new decade. The past ten years have seen a rapid expansion of the village with many new people coming to live here. This is occurring at a time when communications technology makes it easier than ever to establish and maintain contact with one another. Modern communication can help us to control events and in this respect the potential for the future is good. We none of us would want to return to the sanitary conditions of Heckington in the past, nor to the earlier education and welfare systems described in these pages. This book itself is a product of advances in computer technology including the abilty to use the world wide web for research.

Yet although we are all much more in contact with the wider world, we seem paradoxically to be less in contact with our neighbours. There is a danger that the identity of our village could disappear, leaving Heckington a more anonymous and less caring place than it has been in the past. So the reason we have written this book is to try, in some small way, to help everyone who chooses to live here to identify with where we have come from and then perhaps to exercise some control over where we are going as a local community - in other words, to help Heckington to continue its distinctive journey through time.

FURTHER READING
To keep the text readable we have not included footnotes or detailed references. Instead this list includes some of our more important source material and other books for further reading.

CHAPTER 1
The relationship between sea and land is shown in a fascinating set of maps in Bennett S & Bennett N (1993), An Historical Atlas of Lincolnshire, University of Hull Press, Hull, ISBN 0-85958-604-9. General background on archaeology is provided by Hunter J & Ralston I (1999), The Archaeology of Britain, Routledge, London; on landscape a useful starting point is Scholes R (1985), Understanding the Countryside, Moorland Publishing Co., Derbyshire, ISBN 086190-060-X. Further useful information and photographs are in Hoskins WG (1970), The Making of the English Landscape, Penguin, Harmondsworth. Early use of tools is described in Schick KD & Toth N (1995), Making Silent Stones Speak, Phoenix, London. A good introduction to the pottery found when field walking is Barton KJ (1975), Pottery in England, David & Charles, Newton Abbot, ISBN 0-71536702-1. Information about the Heckington tile kilns and the area around the Car Dyke has been published in Simmons BB (1977), Roman Tile Kilns at Heckington, Lincs., Car Dyke Publications No.3, Car Dyke Research Group, Steynings Lane, Swineshead, Lincolnshire. An expert guide to local terms and their derivations is to be found in Healey H (1997), A Fenland Landscape Glossary for Lincolnshire, Lincolnshire Books, Lincoln, ISBN 1-872375-01-4. General background to the history of Roman Britain is in Collingwood RG & Myres JNL (1936), Roman Britain and the English Settlements, Clarendon Press, Oxford.

CHAPTER 2
General background to the history of medieval Britain derives from the texts in the Oxford History of England series; all published at the Clarendon Press, Oxford, in particular for the earlier period Stenton FM (1947), Anglo-Saxon England. Recent opinion on the derivation of the name "Heckington" is to be found in Cameron K (1998), A Dictionary of Lincolnshire Place Names, The English Place Name Society, Nottingham, ISBN 0-904889-58-0. Credit for the research into the story of Richard de Potesgrave is due to Charles Kightly whose unpublished account is available from the Heckington Village Trust. For leading citizens in Heckington at an important point in the middle ages, see the Lincolnshire Lay Subsidy for Heckington (1332) at the Leicester University website on www.le.ac.uk/elh/pot/lincs/hecking.html, while the medieval tax scam has been pieced together out of original records published as McLane BW (1988), The Royal Inquest in Lincolnshire, Lincoln Record Society Vol 78, Boydell Press, Suffolk, ISBN 0-901503-51-7. The background on the feudal system comes from Seebohm F (1883), The English Village Community, Longmans, Green & Co., London.

CHAPTERS 3-5
Some of the detailed content has been built from original manuscripts including: Diocesan Return for 1563, British Museum Harleian MS 618; Hearth Tax Returns, PRO E179 (140/754) 17 Charles II 1665; Hearth Tax Returns, PRO E179 (140/791) 23 Charles II 1671. Also valuable were the handwritten copies of Heckington Wills painstakingly transcribed by Marjorie Woods from the Archives in Lincoln. A typed copy is available for reference from the Heckington Village Trust Useful background reading includes Wheeler WH (1990), A History of the Fens of South Lincolnshire, Paul Watkins, Stamford; Thirsk J (1957), English Peasant Farming: The Agrarian History of Lincolnshire from Tudor to Recent Times, Methuen, London; Trollope E (1999 reprint of 1872 original), Sleaford and the Wapentakes of Flaxwell and Aswardhurn in the County of Lincoln, Heritage Lincolnshire, Heckington; Trevelyan GM (1942), English Social History, Longmans, London; The History of Lincolnshire Series Volumes I-XII, out of print but available from Sleaford Library; Hibbert C (1987), The English: A Social History, Paladin, London. On Dick Turpin many local places lay claim to a connection including York where the following website is based at www.eveningpress.co.uk/york/factfile/yorkhistory/dickturpin/

CHAPTER 6
A mine of local information based around the census of 1870 is to be found in a publication from Heckington Village Trust, Heckington in the Eighteen Seventies. It is now out of print but available through local libraries and the Heckington Village Trust still has a few copies for purchase. The history of the windmill is well described in Pocklington AR (1983), Heckington's Magnificent Eight-Sailed Windmill. Lincolnshire County Council, Lincoln. ISBN 086111-005-7. A wealth of photographic information can be obtained from Heckington 1999 The way we are, ISBN 0-9535362-0-3 by P.Banister & M.Wilkinson and Heckington 2000 times past and present, ISBN 0-9535362-1-1 by P.Banister. Both available at Lincolnshire Libraries and are available for purchase locally. Most of the other information for this chapter came from the local knowledge of the authors of this book, supplemented, we hope, with only the smallest amount of imaginative embellishment.

Index

Symbols

103 High Street 47 & 48
18 Boston Road 47
2 Church Street 47
42 High Street 47
67 and 69 Church Street 47

A

aerial photographs 98 & 99
AGE OF FAITH 19
AGRICULTURE 56
Albion House 47 & 48
Anglo-Saxon 16
Auxiliary Fire Service 122

B

BOSTON ROAD 127
Boston, Sleaford and Midland Counties railway 130
Boy Scouts 94
Bronze Age, 8
Bronze Age 11
BUGGY BELL'S LANE 114
Butts Hill 16

C

CAMERON STREET 114
Car Dyke, 13
Changes in Heckington 100
CHANGING SOCIETY 50
CHURCH STREET 104
CHURCHYARD 119
Civil War 30
Cobham Hall 32
COOK'S CORNER 135
council chamber 127
COWGATE 111
Cromwell's Commonwealth, 30

D

DECOY 39
DICK TURPIN 40
DOMESDAY BOOK 17
DRAINAGE 41

E

EARLIEST SETTLERS 9
EASTGATE 124
EDUCATION 81
Edward II, 23
Edward III 23
ENCLOSURE 42

F

FARMING WAY OF LIFE 18
Feast Tuesday 96
FEUDAL SYSTEM 19
FIELD WALKING 9
Field Walking Techniques 14
flint 10
FLINT-WORKING 12

G

'Garwick' 14
gasworks 112
GLEANING 60

H

HARD TIMES 62
Heckington Bypass 100
HECKINGTON MANOR HOUSE 35
Heckington School 85
Heckington Show 95
HEDGES IN MODERN TIMES 46
Henry VIII' 29
HIGH STREET 135
HOLMES HOUSE 34
Horticultural Society 96
HOUSES 47
HOUSES OF THE POOR 36
Howell 8
'hypocaust' tiles. 13

I

Iron Age 8

K

KILLING THE PIG 107
King Charles 32
KYME ROAD 113

L

LAND 37
Langdale 10
Latimer House 136
LEISURE 64
Littleworth Drove. 14
LIVELIHOODS 63

M

MANOR HOUSE 108
MEDIEVAL HECKINGTON: 16
Michael Cole Sumners. 139

N

NAME OF HECKINGTON 17
No 4 the Green 47 & 48
Norman incomers 17

P

Peacock and Handley's Bank 138
Pearoom. 131
POVERTY 27
PUBS 64

R

RECREATION 64
RELIGION 79
RELIGIOUS LIFE 52
Richard de Potesgrave 20
ROADS 49
ROMAN HECKINGTON 12
Roman settlers, 8
ROYAL VISIT 23

S

SAINT ANDREWS STREET 121
salt making 7
salt-water creeks 7
Samian pottery 13
Saxon burials 16
Saxon farmers 17
Saxons 17
SCHOOL CONCERT 1908 86
SECOND WORLD WAR 90
Sir John Broke 32
Sir John Cobham 32
SLEAFORD ROAD 140
STATION COMPLEX 129
STUARTS: 27

T

TAX SCAM 25
Temperance Hall 135
Temperance Revival 65
'tesserae' 13
The Beck 8
THE COTTAGER 61
THE MILL 129
The Red House 47
TITHE BARN 31
TRANSPORT 87
TUDORS 27

V

VICTORIAN HECKINGTON 56
Viking invaders 16
VILLAGE GREEN 140
VILLAGE LIVELIHOODS 54
village show 95

W

WALK ROUND THE VILLAGE 102
Wash Dyke 8
WEALTH 27
WHITE HORSE 108
Wido de Creon. 17
William Little' 66
WINKHILL MANOR 34